KUNG-FU
MONTHLY

THE ARCHIVE SERIES

WHO KILLED BRUCE LEE

BY THE EDITORS OF
KUNG-FU MONTHLY

COMPILED AND EDITED BY
CARL FOX

PIT WHEEL PRESS
BARNSLEY

Published by
PIT WHEEL PRESS LIMITED
www.pitwheelpress.com

Copyright © 2025 Pit Wheel Press Limited. All Right Reserved. No part of this book may be reproduced, scanned or distributed in any printed or electronic form without permission.

WHO KILLED BRUCE LEE

Copyright © 1978 by H. Bunch Associates Ltd. (except where copyright on certain photographic material already exists). This publication or any parts thereof may not be reproduced in any form whatsoever without permission in writing from the copyright proprietor.

A Pit Wheel Press edition, published by special arrangement with Dennis Publishing, London.

First Printing 1978
Revised Edition 2025

Printed in the United Kingdom
ISBN 978-1-915414-33-5

ACKNOWLEDGEMENTS

I would like to thank the following people for their help and participation in the making of this book:

James Bishop **Matthew Robins**
John Little **Carlotta Serantoni**
James McKeown **Andrew Staton**

Special Thanks
Marcos Ocana

CREDITS

Original 1978 Edition

PHOTO CREDITS

Golden Harvest Films, Warner Bros Films & Chester Maydole

The Kung-Fu Monthly Archive Series

Research, Editing, Layout & Design
Carl Fox

Editorial Assistance
George Fox

Photograph Acknowlegements
Kung-Fu Monthly & Carl Fox

Kung-Fu Monthly Collage Image
Copyright © 2025 Carl Fox

KUNG-FU MONTHLY

THE ARCHIVE SERIES
WHO KILLED BRUCE LEE?
CHAPTERS

	ABOUT THE KFM ARCHIVE SERIES	11
	FOREWORD BY MARCOS OCANA	15
	INTRODUCTION (2024)	23
	INTRODUCTION (1978)	25
01	WRITING ON THE WALL	29
02	THE KING IS DEAD	41
03	STICKS, STONES & BAD FENG SHUI	57
04	GAME OF DEATH	75
	EPILOGUE	101
	THE BOB BAKER LETTERS	107

KUNG-FU
MONTHLY

THE ARCHIVE SERIES
ABOUT THE SERIES

WHO KILLED BRUCE LEE

Kung-Fu Monthly is a name synonymous with Bruce Lee, not only in the United Kingdom but throughout the world. It is a legend in its own right and a brand immediately recognisable by not only the font but also the famous "flying man" logo.

The popularity of the magazine at the peak of the Kung Fu Craze in the 1970s was unrivalled and its success was almost entirely down to pure luck.

Legend has it that *Kung-Fu Monthly* began life as a gamble by underground comic book publisher Felix Dennis after questioning a queue of kids outside a Soho cinema, waiting to see *Enter the Dragon* in early 1974. On paper, the idea seemed to serve the then-current trend of Bruce Lee and was deemed to have a shelf life of three to six months but a year after its launch, *Kung-Fu Monthly* had become the biggest-selling Bruce Lee magazine in the world.

After the demise of the Official Bruce Lee Fan Club in 1976, *Kung-Fu Monthly* launched their own. The KFM Bruce Lee Society ran for thirty quarterly newsletters from 1976 to 1983 and at the time of closing, had seen over five thousand eager Bruce Lee fans become members throughout its tenure, with the formidable Pam Hadden at the forefront throughout its seven active years.

Kung-Fu Monthly and The Bruce Lee Society were jointly responsible for the UK's first Bruce Lee Convention held on May 19th 1979 and the first Bruce Lee Film Festival held on December 1st 1979.

Kung-Fu Monthly and later *Personal Computer World*, had turned H. Bunch Associates from an underground publisher on the verge of bankruptcy to a publishing powerhouse, eventually becoming Dennis Publishing, named after its founder, Felix Dennis.

That leads us to today.

In February 2021, I approached Dennis Publishing with an idea for a project that I'd thought of doing for many years - scan, convert, edit and compile all seventy-nine issues of the iconic *Kung-Fu Monthly* magazine into book form, in order to present it to a new audience, as well as preserve its place in history.

It was the longest-running dedicated Bruce Lee magazine of its kind anywhere in the world (by frequency and circulation) and I wanted to pay homage to that. Such was its success and popularity that it was licensed throughout the world; in fourteen countries and in eleven languages. That doesn't even take into account the non-official bootlegs which appeared in China and Turkey. Nothing has matched it before or since. It truly has stood the test of time and having done so, has reached legendary status.

Kung-Fu Monthly is a snapshot of a time long gone; a time which the original fans remember with fondness and a time which new fans will hopefully discover.

The *Kung-Fu Monthly Archive Series* is dedicated to Felix Dennis and everyone associated with the magazine; not just the staff but also the fans, who would buy copies of the magazines in their millions over its lifetime and help cement the publication's place in British Pop Culture history.

Special thanks must also go to Carlotta Serantoni at Dennis Publishing for her assistance in allowing this project to go ahead.

Carl Fox
February 2022

KUNG-FU MONTHLY

THE ARCHIVE SERIES
WHO KILLED BRUCE LEE
FOREWORD

WHO KILLED BRUCE LEE

After the night of July 20, 1973, the media, the insurance companies, the fans... began a quest for answers to try to clarify one of the biggest mysteries in the history of cinema: How did Bruce Lee die? What or, as the title of this book suggests, Who Killed Bruce Lee? When it was first published in 1978, the death of the Little Dragon was still shrouded in mystery. All kinds of theories were circulating, each more far-fetched than the last, and the official inquest had not clarified anything. The very title of this work implied that it was something provoked and Bruce was simply taken out of the way. People needed answers and someone to blame, and for five years actress Betty Ting Pei had been in the center of all their targets. But was she really responsible for his death? Was it his partner, producer Raymond Chow? Is there really someone we can point the finger at and blame?

KFM writer and co-author of King of Kung Fu, Don Atyeo, travelled to Hong Kong in search of answers, only to be faced with the harsh reality that people either knew nothing or did not want to damage the image of the city's "Number 1 Son". This led him to largely review the news published by the press in 1973, which collected part of the testimonies of some of the witnesses at the inquest to try to clarify the causes of his death and, together with some interviews, attempt to put together the pieces of an almost impossible puzzle where, as he himself admits, he aims to accurately recreate the terrible circumstances of his death.

This approach to the facts was accepted in 1978 and helped many fans understand the mindset of the time, the level of obsession there was with Bruce Lee, what had made him a cult figure and why his loss had caused such a stir. But five decades later it is impossible not to feel that bitter aftertaste that the book could no longer contribute anything new... Or could it?

When Carl Fox decided to reissue the *Kung-Fu Monthly* series of books, he not only did a great job of restoration by scanning and cleaning the original documents. He also made the smart decision to incorporate new elements that could not only preserve the vintage flavor of the 70s, but also attract a current audience by giving the reader another perspective through contributions based on recent research and discoveries.

In this new revised and expanded edition of *Who Killed Bruce Lee*, Carl Fox brings to the forefront a crucial fact that, surprisingly, had remained hidden for 50 years. An event that on July 5, 2021 changed overnight the way of seeing Bruce Lee and his perhaps no longer so mysterious death. When the Bob Baker letters, Lee's friend and student in Oakland, were made public, their numerous allusions to Bruce Lee's consumption of very diverse substances did not leave any fan of the Little Dragon indifferent. Disappointment, frustration... were largely the main feelings left in the fans.

Now in Who Killed Bruce Lee, the old and the new come together to offer a much broader perspective of the event that has generated the most debates about his figure since that fateful night of the 20th of July 1973. Is it possible that a new name could be added to the list of those possibly responsible for his death, and that name could be that of Bruce Lee himself?

It is up to you the reader to draw your own conclusions.

Marcos Ocaña
January 2025

Marcos Ocaña (b. 1974 Madrid, Spain) has been a martial artist since the age of twelve and a primary school teacher since 1996.

In 2000 he created the forum In the Spirit of Bruce Lee. He has lectured in Madrid, Barcelona and Malaga; and is the author of the audio commentary tracks for Bruce Lee's films on DVD and Blu-ray in Spain.

He has published over 200 articles and since 2007, is the Chief Editor of Bruce Lee Mania magazine, which he directed between 2017 and 2020.

Marcos is the author of the acclaimed Bruce Lee books T*he Man Behind The Legend* (2003), The Bamboo Warrior (2010), *Memories from Dominican Republic* (2015), *Unlimited* (2018), *The Silent Flute* (2019) and *The Death of Bruce Lee* (2020-22).

He is widely considered to be one of the foremost Bruce Lee historians.

Bruce Lee's death has been shrouded in mystery for decades. Through official forensic reports, medical analysis, and witness statements made at the trial and before the police, many published here for the first time, this book constitutes the most detailed study ever conducted regarding the circumstances surrounding the untimely death of The Little Dragon. Delve into one of the most controversial milestones in cinema history.

LA MUERTE DE / THE DEATH OF
BRUCE LEE

MARCOS OCAÑA RIZO

TOTALMENTE BILINGÜE

FULLY BILINGUAL

YA DISPONIBLE

NOW AVAILABLE

REVISED AND EXTENDED EDITION

Información y pedidos / info & orders
bld1970@yahoo.es

KUNG-FU MONTHLY

THE ARCHIVE SERIES
WHO KILLED BRUCE LEE

KUNG-FU MONTHLY

THE ARCHIVE SERIES
WHO KILLED BRUCE LEE
INTRODUCTION (2024)

WHO KILLED BRUCE LEE

Here we are, almost fifty-two years after the passing of Bruce Lee, the undisputed King of Kung Fu.

Whilst replicating the original content of the time, *The Kung-Fu Monthly Archive Series* has strived to present additional information when it has been available. I did it with *The Wisdom of Bruce Lee* with a history of the lost KFM book and an interview with the original author, Roger Hutchinson. With that in mind, I wanted to do that with *Who Killed Bruce Lee*.

The publication of *Who Killed Bruce Lee* was controversial at the time, presenting conspiracy theories and showing Lee in his coffin. I did consider omitting that photo in this edition, however I decided to leave it in as the aim of the series is to present the books in their entirety, no matter how difficult the subject may be. History cannot be undone or erased.

With that in mind, I have added an article that I wrote in the wake of the infamous Bob Baker letters being discovered in 2021. The article I wrote went unpublished; mainly because the publishers that expressed interest in publishing it, wanted me to change it to push a more sensationalised agenda. They wanted Bruce Lee portrayed as a helpless junkie whereas I always wanted to present a balanced view of Bruce Lee as a human being, flaws and all.

Some people still want to hold onto the view of Saint Bruce and cannot fathom their life with Bruce being anything other than perfection; whether that be as an actor, as a martial artist or as a human being. After all, Bruce Lee famously stated to Canadian broadcaster Pierre Berton that he wanted to be thought of not as an actor or martial artist; but as a human being.

I did not want to delve too much into Bruce Lee's death. The article on the Bob Baker letters was added because it needed to be; you can't omit the most significant discovery about Lee's death since the original book was published.

When I was putting this book together, I looked at who I would like to ask to write the foreword; in the past, Chris Kent, Tim Tackett, Martin O'Neill, and Bey Logan had done the honours. For *Who Killed Bruce Lee*, I asked the renowned Spanish author, Marcos Ocana, to contribute a foreword. Marcos is a prolific author in his native Spain, writing many extraordinarily-researched books on Bruce Lee but there is one book in particular that delves into the exact nature of this book - *The Death of Bruce Lee*. *The Death of Bruce Lee* presents the evidence of the past fifty-something years including documents and testimonies of the original autopsy and inquest so I thought it fitting to ask Marcos to write the foreword to *Who Killed Bruce Lee*. His book, *The Death of Bruce Lee* is another reason why I did not want to add too much of my own writing to this book as I could never have done anything as expansive as what Marcos has achieved with his book.

So thank you, Marcos and thank you, the fans, for accepting Bruce Lee for what he wanted to be remembered for; as a human being, warts and all.

Carl Fox
26th December 2024

COLLECTOR'S EDITION

WHO KILLED BRUCE LEE?

Scores of photos of The Master in action

By the editors of Kung-Fu Monthly

KUNG-FU
MONTHLY

THE ARCHIVE SERIES
WHO KILLED BRUCE LEE
INTRODUCTION (1978)

WHO KILLED BRUCE LEE

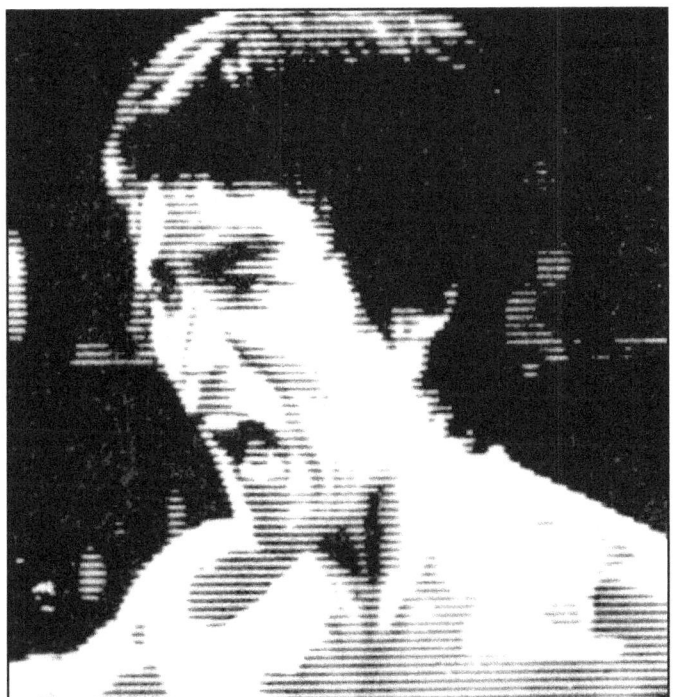

The circumstances surrounding Bruce Lee's death in 1973 unleashed a storm of discontent which swept across Asia, and throughout the rest of the world, leaving in its wake a tangled welter of claims and counterclaims regarding the causes of his dying. His physical fitness was too well known for people to accept that he might have simply died of natural causes.

Now, five years after his death, the trail of information has grown road weary. Bruce Lee was the biggest film star ever to come out of Asia and information about his life, and especially his death, is still in great international demand. With writers still clambering for exclusive knowledge about Bruce Lee, the unscrupulous of Hong Kong are only too willing to exploit this demand, only too willing to supply their own "exclusive information" at a very high price.

It took a full month of patient digging through the archives and alleyways of Hong Kong to produce the material for this book. Often exciting new information would surface only to learn that the informant had never known Bruce Lee. New "facts" continued to come to light and wherever possible, each was checked against two independent sources before being accepted or discarded. But as time passes and memory dims, the stories about Bruce Lee's life and death, survive and grow. His legend exceeds his life.

It is impossible to know and feel the exact mood of Hong Kong during the time of Bruce Lee's death. And certainly some of what is written in this book must be inflated, some not exactly as it happened, but this book attempts to accurately recreate the terrible circumstances of his death and the tragic effect it had upon those who knew and loved him. This is the way we found it happened.

CHAPTER ONE

WRITING ON THE WALL

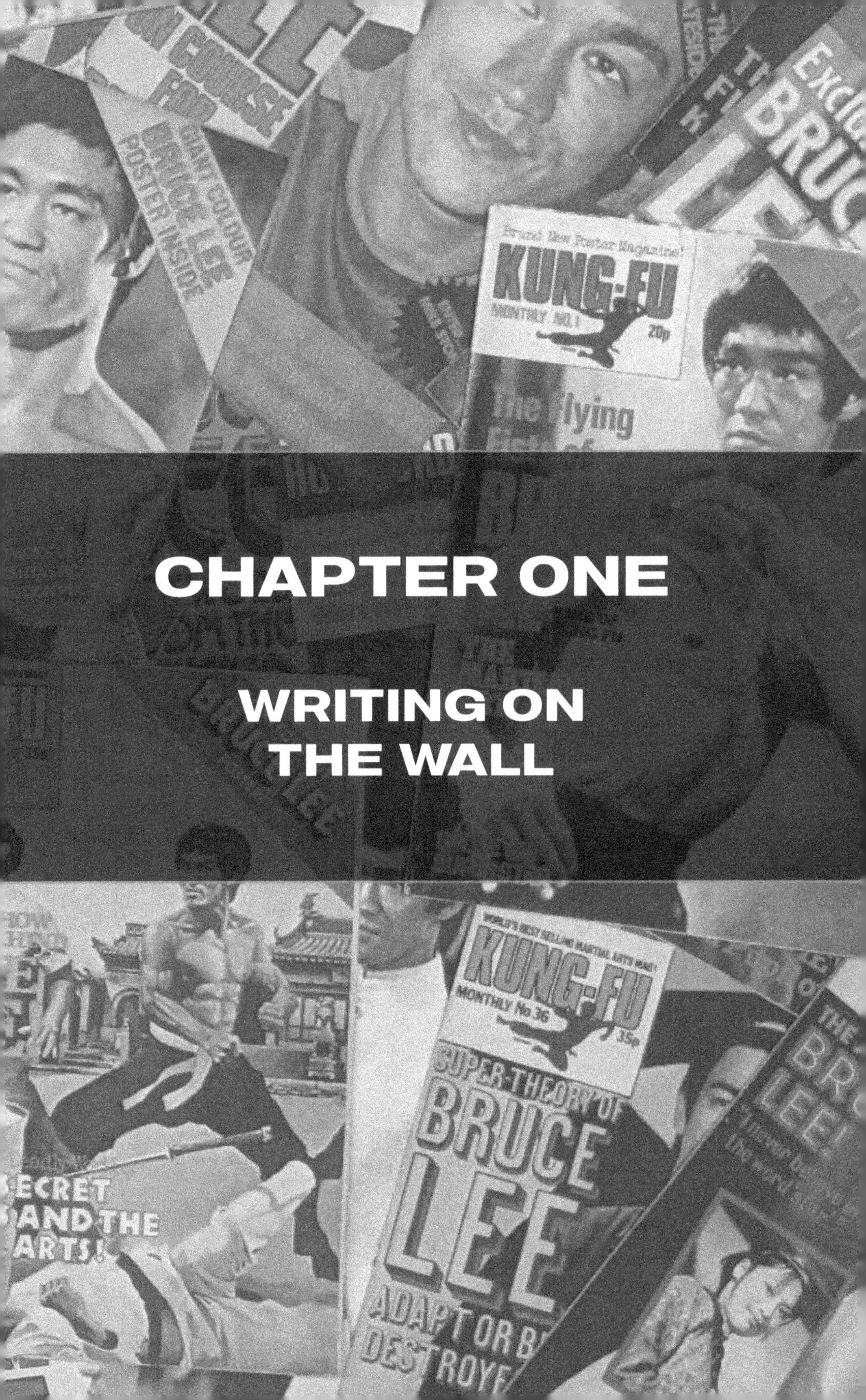

"First there were breathing noises, then they stopped. There was a series of convulsions. The entire body was involved in this motion, but the upper limbs gave us the most difficulty because he was very strong and was difficult to control. It took us one and a half hours to make Lee conscious."

WHO KILLED BRUCE LEE

Prior to and during filming of his Hollywood epic, *Enter the Dragon*, pressure on Bruce Lee was building to near intolerable levels. The strain of "overnight" stardom is a cliched syndrome in the entertainment business, but real enough for all that, effecting different personalities in a variety of ways. Some it drives into recluses, like Greta Garbo and Bob Dylan, while for others it provides a welcome platform before the hungry eyes of the world. Lee, it split in two.

On the one hand, public adulation was the vital ingredient necessary to support Lee's dynamic ego. In Hong Kong he lived out his superhero identity to the full. His house in Kowloon Tong was a latter day mansion; he drove a HK$41,000 scarlet Mercedes convertible; he ordered a Rolls Royce with a gold nameplate. In press photographs, his arms were continually embracing beautiful and delectable Hong Kong actresses, and for weekends, he had James Coburn and other big time names over to stay. "Having money doesn't solve all your problems," he told one interviewer, "but it sure beats not having money." "When he felt like reassuring himself that he really was Bruce Lee," says Andre Morgan of Golden Harvest films, "he'd just walk down the street and he knew everyone would be going 'Bruce Lee,' 'Bruce Lee!'"

But fame exacts its own price and Lee was in difficulty keeping up the instalments. He says it all himself in an interview with Mike Plane: "It's ironic, but we all strive to become wealthy and famous. Once you're there it's not all rosy. There's hardly a place in Hong Kong where I can go to without being stared at or without people asking for autographs. Whenever I go to public places like a restaurant I try to sneak in without being detected. I'll go directly to a corner table and quickly sit down, facing the wall with my back to the crowd. I keep my head low while I'm eating. No, I'm not crazy - I only look it. If I'm recognised I'm dead because I can't eat with the hand that I have used to sign autographs.

"And I'm not one of those guys who can brush people off. I feel that if I can take just a second and make someone happy, why not do it now? Now I understand why stars like Steve (McQueen) and Big Lew (Jabber) avoid public places.

"In the beginning, I didn't mind all the publicity I was getting. But soon it got to be a headache answering the same questions over and over again, posing for photos and forcing a smile."

Lee had never been much of a party-goer, avoiding the usual social gatherings that are an integral part of the Hong Kong film industry as often as he could. "I'm not that kind of cat," said Lee. "I don't drink or smoke and these events are many times senseless. I don't like to wear stuffy clothes and be at places where everyone is trying to impress each other. I'm not saying I'm modest, I just rather like to be around a few friends and talk informally about boxing and the martial arts."

But as his popularity increased he withdrew further and further into himself, sometimes spending days on end in his study which had been fitted out with a refrigerator, television and shelves of martial and philosophical books. Although always retaining a small coterie of intimates, one by one Lee's close friends were abandoned, often hurt and offended by the barriers, both emotional and physical, he built around himself. At one time he had been willing to endorse his colleagues' films - for a budding star named Unicorn Chan, he even made a walk-on appearance in the movie *Fist of Unicorn* - but now he refused. Raymond Chow became his only constant companion, and even he wasn't immune from Lee's occasional outbursts. When the Golden Harvest fan magazine ran an

THE KUNG-FU MONTHLY ARCHIVE SERIES

article on the Chow/Lee relationship, Lee responded angrily: "The article puts forth a notion that I am a brainless child who relies solely on Raymond but I am not. Instead I am my own boss and I have as much brains as others." Later, he denied there was any split in the friendship, saying, "We are as friendly as ever," but the incident serves to illustrate Lee's growing, if spasmodic, paranoia and fear of exploitation.

Besides alienating many of his friends, Lee also grew wary of appearing in public. When returning to his old school, Saint Francis Xavier College, to present the Sports Day prizes, he introduced Bob Baker, the co-star of *Fist of Fury,* as his "bodyguard." During the ceremony, a door banged shut behind the stage and Lee immediately leaped to the ground, visibly shaken. Later, Lee showed the school principal, Brother Gregory, a bag which he was carrying. Inside, he said, was a gun. Who or what Lee might have been afraid of we shall examine in a later chapter, but it is a sad irony that one of the most lethal men in the world, a champion of self-defence, felt it necessary to carry a gun for protection.

But by this time Lee's life was not his own - it was the common property of his millions of Chinese admirers, and the more he sought seclusion, the more he was hounded. In the early days Lee had been the constant darling of the Eastern press, free with candid interviews and shots of himself on and off the set. Now, however, the press watched him like a hawk, waiting for any slip in his jealously guarded superhero image.

Andre Morgan: "It was the old story of the Italians making their living by photographing Jackie Kennedy or Elizabeth Taylor. There were guys here who used to follow him around, taking photographs and selling them to magazines. Every little incident became something very big. He had a fight with a dresser at a TV studio and it made front page headlines for the next three days. Abdul Kareem Jabbar - a black muslim - had a house rented out to mlack muslims in Washington and there was an inter-tribal fight and all

THE KUNG-FU MONTHLY ARCHIVE SERIES

these black muslims were wiped out. The front page headline in Hong Kong was: "BRUCE LEE LINKED TO MASS MURDER." You read the article and it turns out that a man who was in Hong Kong last week filming has a house in America which is rented to some people who were wiped out last night. That was the link, and that was the sort of way newspapers treated Lee."

The really big split between Lee and the newspapers came when he walked out of a television studio one day into the waiting hordes, of Hong Kong's paparazzi. He posed for shots but they demanded more. He refused and angrily told them to leave him alone. There was a scuffle. In the next day's press there were headlines about how Lee had mistreated cameramen.

This distrust between star and newsmen was further aggravated after a Hong Kong evening daily, *The Star*, ran an article quoting a student of Ip Man who claimed he had seen Lee knocked down by an opponent during training. Lee, his "invincible" reputation threatened, took out a writ against the paper. Star owner and editor Graham Jenkins, a tough, hard-bitten Australian who has been bossing newspapers up and down the Far East for decades, maintains that Lee had threatened the Star's informant and had forced him to change his story. Later, Lee would be the key figure in the biggest scoop of the paper's history.

Undoubtedly the Hong Kong press pushed Lee, but on many occasions it was his own extravagant ego and violent temper which conspired to thrust his neck into the unwelcome noose of publicity. Appearing on a Hong Kong television programme one evening as part of a panel of martial artists, Lee and his fellow panellists were invited by a middle

WHO KILLED BRUCE LEE

aged member of the audience to attempt to push him off balance. Each of Lee's colleagues tried in turn to dislodge the man after he had adopted a fighting stance, and one by one they failed. Finally, only Lee remained to try. Taunted by the man to "have a go," Lee stood up and slammed him in the face with his fist, knocking him to the floor. When asked later why he had resorted to such aggressive behaviour Lee replied, "I don't push, I punch." As a lesson in the freedoms of Jeet Kune Do it was perfect, but on television it appeared an ugly and unnecessarily violent incident and the media pounced on it. Ever since *The Big Boss*, Lee and Lo Wei, his former director, had engaged in a bitter, feuding relationship, poisoned by ego and "artistic differences". In July 1973, this relationship exploded in a welter of sensational headlines. Angered by the thought that Lo Wei was taking credit for the success of his first films, Lee boiled over in rage at the old man as he sat in a Golden Harvest sound studio. When Lo Wei's wife objected to the torrent of abuse heaped upon her husband, Lee threatened the director with physical harm. The police were called and the matter was not resolved until Lee had taken the extraordinary step of signing a piece of paper which stated: "I, Bruce Lee, will leave Lo Wei alone." The newspapers made a meal out of the flare-up and it left a nasty taste in many a fan's mouth.

There were other incidents, many of which the press did not see. During the filming of *Enter the Dragon*, Lee fought with script writer Michael Allen and with producer Fred Weintraub. There was also much ill feeling, going way beyond the bounds of friendly rivalry, between Lee and his co-star, Bob Wall, a former U.S. Professional Karate champion. In the scene where Wall lunges at Lee with the bottles, he held onto them too long during

WHO KILLED BRUCE LEE

one rehearsal and sliced Lee's hand, putting him out of action for many days. Friends of Wall told me in Hong Kong that it might not have been entirely an accident.

All of these temper tantrums with press, friends and colleagues can doubtless be attributed to the enormous tension weighing on Lee at that time. He desperately wanted to be a film star on an equal footing with Coburn and McQueen and his impatience with the frustrations and obstacles that blocked his path are legendary. When introduced to a guest at a party who failed to recognise him, Lee thrust out his hand, rudely turned his head aside and snapped, "Bruce Lee... Movie Star!" It was behaviour like this that earned Lee many enemies in Hong Kong, besides warning his closer friends that the strain of success was beginning to take a heavy physical and emotional toll.

Built like the Great Wall of China, ever since he sat at his parents' dinner table as a 13-year-old boy, pounding his fist against the stool, Lee's body had been his pride and obsession. He spent hours each morning on a rigorous training schedule which included a three mile run. Often he would wake during the night and slip out of bed to practice Kung-Fu in the living room, leaping over tables and chairs and shadow boxing the curtains. He owned an electrical device which, when strapped around his waist, slowed down his blood circulation, forcing him to work much harder to complete his exercises.

The Kowloon Tong house was equipped with a college size gymnasium lined with mirrors to allow him to observe his own movements in training. He avoided restaurant food and lived on a diet of raw beef, eggs and milk mixed together in a blender, together with many glasses of fruit and vegetable juice. Lee trained as if every fight might be his last, as

THE KUNG-FU MONTHLY ARCHIVE SERIES

if his life depended on his fitness, which in a sense it did. On the Golden Harvest lot, when he wasn't working he would still saunter around stripped to the waist, wearing only his Chinese fighting trousers. He even had the sweat glands removed from under his armpits so that he would look better on camera. In a matter of months, he dropped from 140lbs to 120lbs, and it worried him.

On the afternoon of May 10th 1973, while laying down the soundtrack for *Enter the Dragon* in one of the Golden Harvest dubbing rooms, Lee's body finally failed him.

Raymond Chow: "I was working in my office and one of my empolyees rushed in and said a doctor was needed as Lee had collapsed. Lee had been working in the dubbing studios and I rushed into the studio. I saw he had breathing trouble and he was shaking. I called Dr. Langford at the Baptist Hospital and he told me to rush Lee to hospital immediately."

Dr. Langford, an American, said later that when Lee was brought in he was "very near death." "First there were breathing noises, then they stopped. There was a series of convulsions. The entire body was involved in this motion, but the upper limbs gave us the most difficulty because he was very strong and was difficult to control. It took us one and a half hours to make Lee conscious."

When Lee did come out of the coma, Langford described it as "quite dramatic." "First he was able to move a bit, then he opened his eyes, then he made some sign, but he could not speak. He recognised his wife and made signs of recognition. Later, he was able to speak, but it was slurred, different from the usual way he talked. By the time he was transferred to another hospital, he was able to remember aloud and joke."

Hong Kong neurosurgeon Dr. Peter Wu, who also examined Lee, wanted to give him a brain test, but Lee refused the later flew to Los Angeles where he was examined by a team of doctors led by Dr. David Reisbord. Lee's collapse, concluded Dr. Reisbord, was "a convulsion disorder, a major kind of epilepsy" brought on by an unknown cause. He prescribed for Lee a drug called Dilantin, commonly used by epileptics.

During these troubled times, movie offers had continued to pour into the Golden Harvest offices. MGM wanted Lee to co-star opposite Elvis Presley (himself a martial arts disciple); Carlo Ponti wanted him to co-star with Sophia Loren, and Warner Bros. had twelve new scripts ready with hopes that Bruce could manage at least five of them. James Coburn and 20th Century Fox were anxious to finally make *The Silent Flute*. On top of all this, Lee had been offered two movies in Hungary which, according to one magazine article, would have made him the highest paid actor in the world.

While considering these offers, Lee returned to the planning and scripting of *Game of Death*. Former James Bond, Australian actor George Lazenby, who had seen a Lee movie in America and had "caught the next plane out to Hong Kong," was eager to work with Lee. Eventually, Warner Bros. came through with an offer Lee couldn't refuse: $100,000 a year for as long as either he or Linda should live on completion of one of the five proffered scripts. "Frankly speaking, I am interested in this scheme," he told *The China Mail* in an article on June 28th headlined, "BRUCE LEE SCOOPS A SUPERSTAR SALARY." "It gives me security in the years ahead and makes taxation much easier. Besides, it doesn't bar me from working with any other studio." And then, with a laugh, he added: "I have great confidence in the studio - I think it will outlive me."

CHAPTER TWO

THE KING IS DEAD

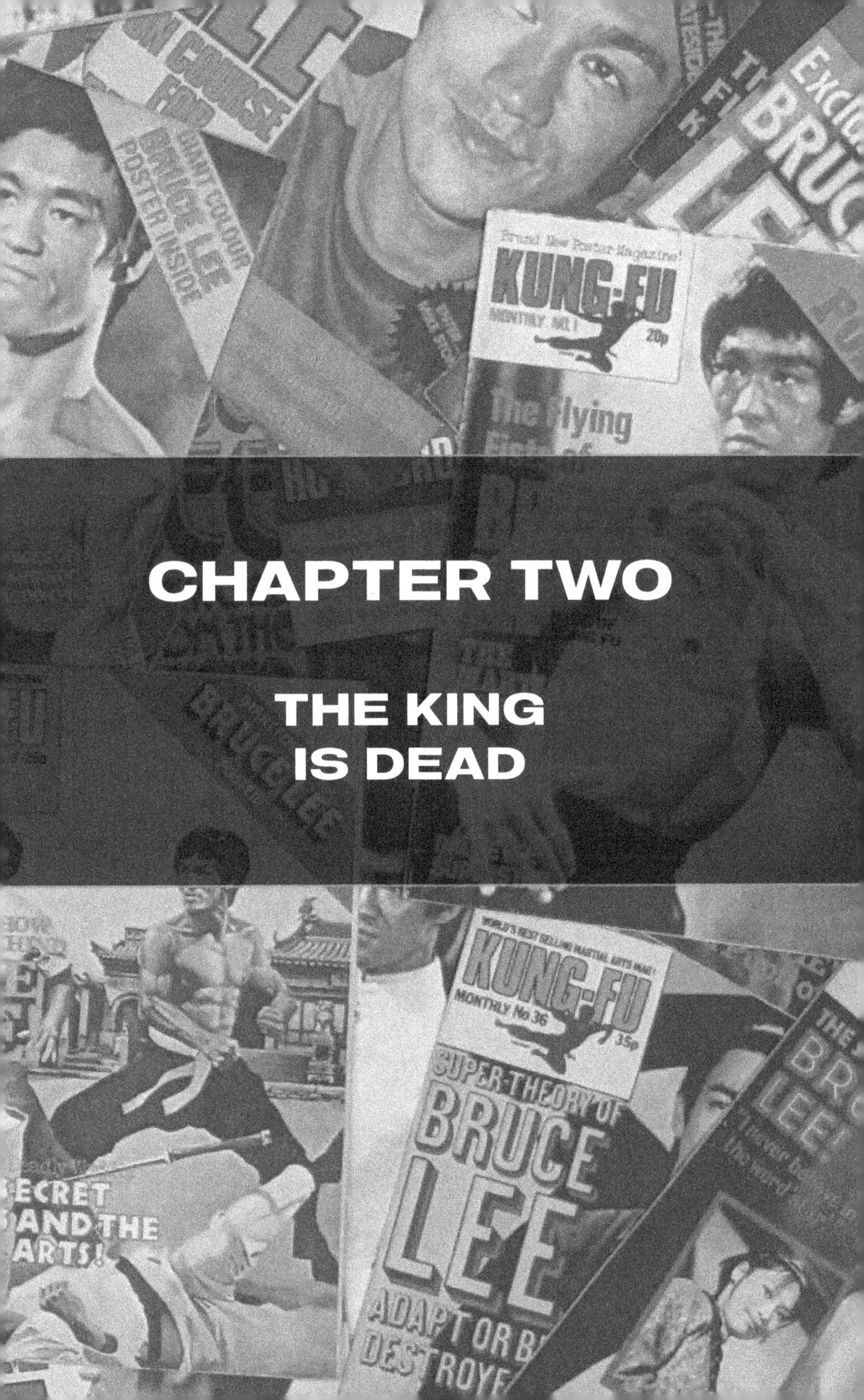

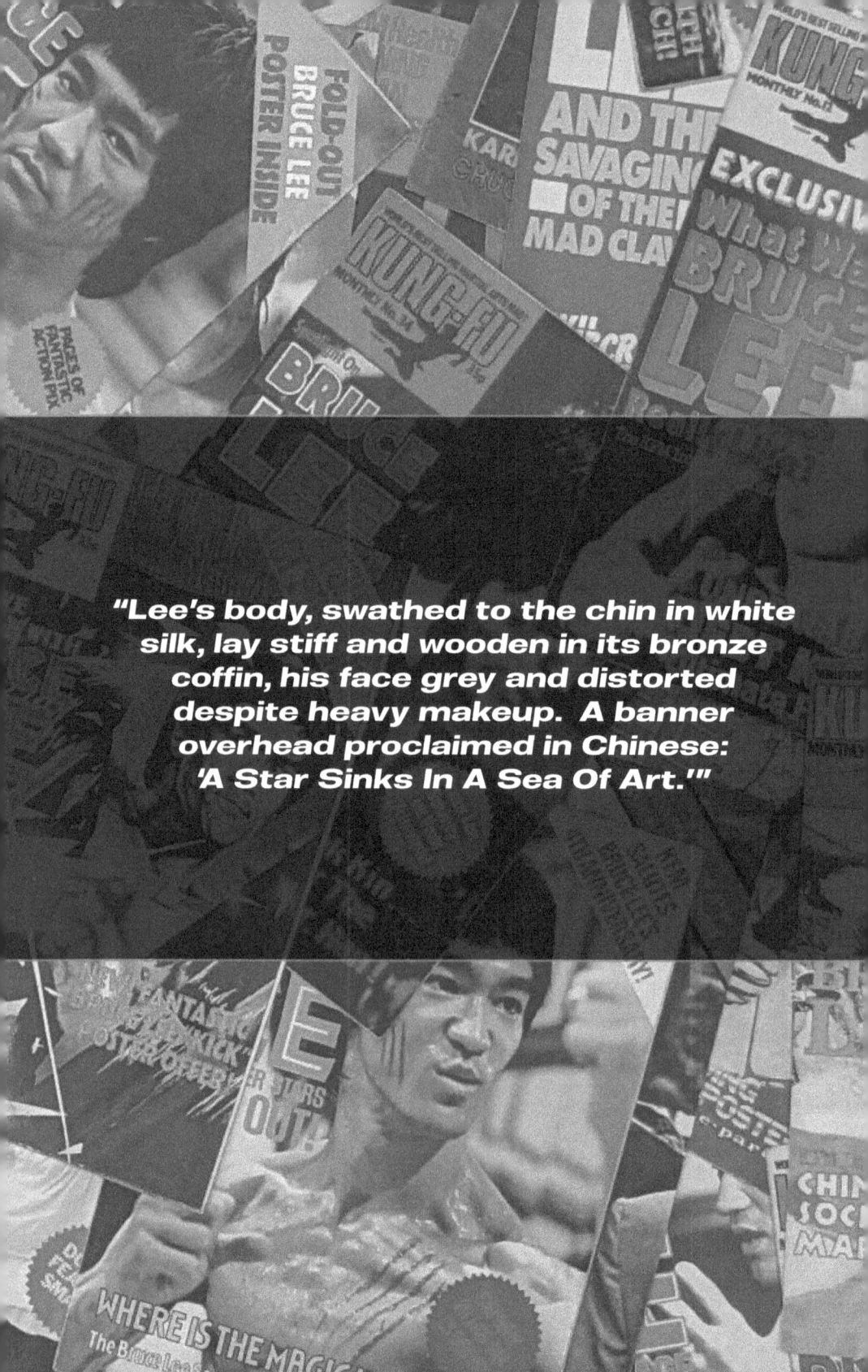

"Lee's body, swathed to the chin in white silk, lay stiff and wooden in its bronze coffin, his face grey and distorted despite heavy makeup. A banner overhead proclaimed in Chinese: 'A Star Sinks In A Sea Of Art.'"

WHO KILLED BRUCE LEE

Sometime close to 8.00 p.m., on the night of July 20th 1973, Bruce Lee went to bed complaining of a headache. The question of whose bed and at what address need not concern us now, although at a later stage, the exact location of his retirement would form a cornerstone to the sordid speculation and intrigue surrounding Lee's last hours. Discovered barely breathing and with no discernable pulse, Lee was rushed more dead than alive to Hong Kong's Queen Elizabeth Hospital, following a bedside examination by a local doctor, Dr. Chu Phohwye. When asked later why he had not sent Lee to the nearby Baptist Hospital, Dr. Chu replied: "I spent at least ten minutes trying to revive him. When he did not show any signs of improvement, it did not occur to me that time was of great importance." On his arrival at approximately 10.30 p.m., Queen Elizabeth doctors fought in vain to pull him out of the coma, using oxygen and heart massage. Linda and Raymond Chow waited silently outside the ward until at 11.30 p.m. Chow stepped through the hospital's main doors to tell waiting reporters: "He's gone."

At the age of 32, the "fittest man in the world" was dead. It seemed impossible. "Why is it always the good guys who go first?" asked George Lazenby. No one had an answer.

It is difficult to overstate the impact of Lee's death on Chinese communities throughout the Far East. In Hong Kong the next morning, stunned commuters were halted in their daily trek to the city centre by the bold headlines screaming from every news stand: "BRUCE LEE IS DEAD." Almost every newspaper in the colony published a special memorial issue and the Chinese language press doubled and tripled its circulation as readers scrambled for souvenir copies.

In other countries, many fans simply refused to believe that Lee was really dead. An article published by *The China Mail* reported that Malaysians in Penang believed the story to be merely a macabre publicity stunt for *Game of Death*. "The fans have been entering heated arguments over the issue and even placing bets," said the report.

World news coverage that morning of the previous night's events was based on two major sources; the first, a statement attributed to Raymond Chow claiming that Lee had collapsed after walking in the gardens of his Kowloon Tong home with Linda, and the second, a hospital report to the effect that although doctors had discovered Lee's brain to be grossly swollen, they were baffled as to what had brought on the seizure.

On the face of it, the story seemed reasonable enough, a fatal repetition of Lee's collapse two months earlier in the Golden Harvest studio. No doubt there would be an autopsy which would confirm he had died from natural causes and that would be an end to the whole tragic affair. If anyone thought differently on the morning of July 21st, either they were keeping it to themselves or their voices were lost in the rush of grief and sympathy for his young widow and children. Within a few short days however, should any coroner have been rash enough to endorse a finding of death through natural causes, it is probably that the people of Hong Kong would have stormed his courthouse.

On July 24th, *The Star* splashed across its front page the sensational news that Lee had been rushed to hospital not from his Cumberland Road home, but from the apartment of a sultry young actress by the name of Betty Ting Pei. "BRUCE LEE SHOCK," blared *The Star*, quoting an ambulance official who confirmed that Lee had been taken from 67 Beacon Hill Road, Kowloon Tong - Betty Ting's home. Raymond Chow, trapped in an uncomfortable spotlight of publicity, dropped from sight like a stone, leaving pretty Miss Ting, a Taiwanese starlet, to face the angry press alone.

WHO KILLED BRUCE LEE

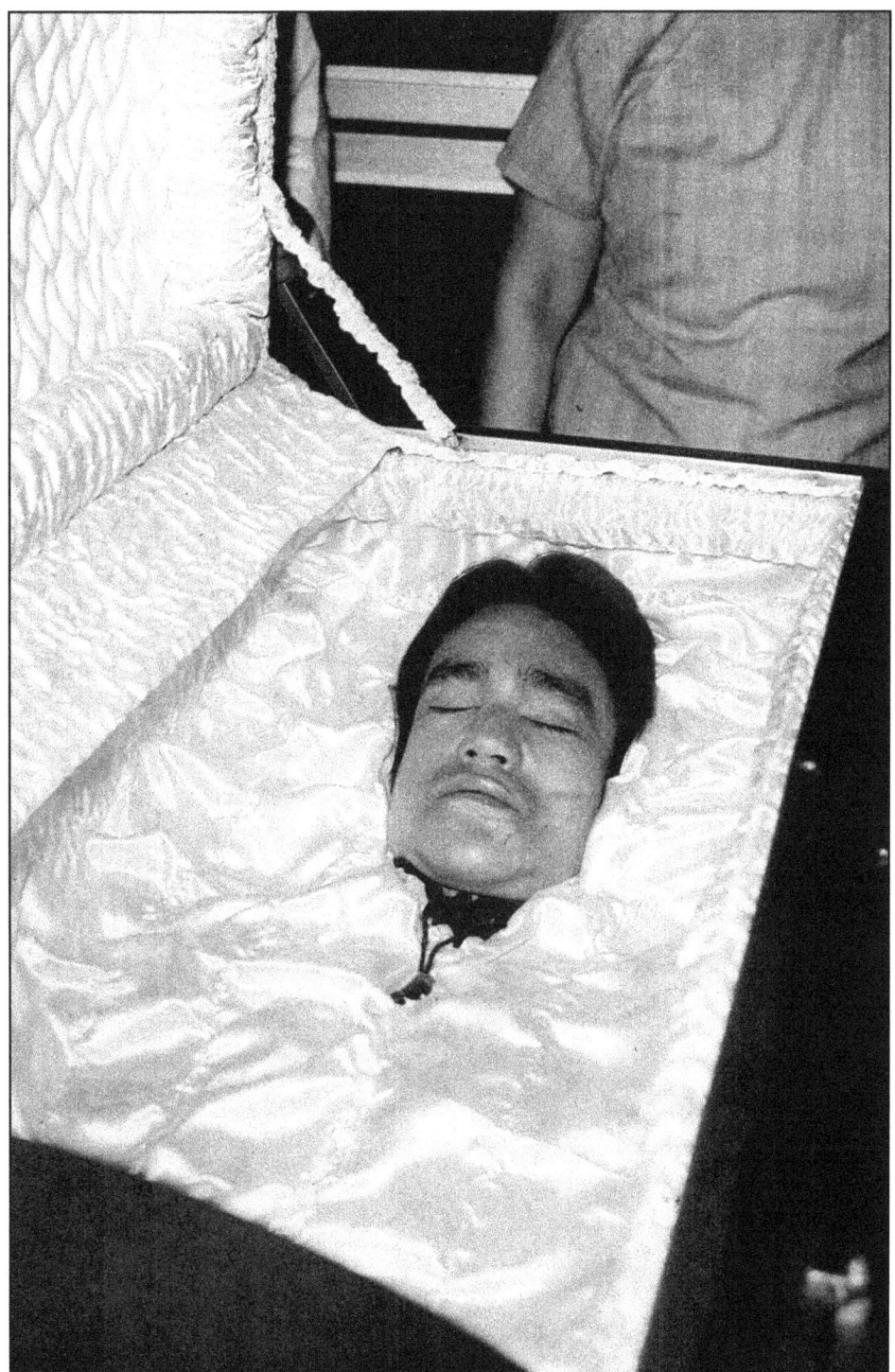

Flustered and defensive, she made the foolish mistake of compounding a lie. "On Friday night when he died I was not at home - I had gone out with my mother," she snapped at reporters. "I last met him several months ago when we came across each other in the street." Lee's friends and colleagues, including his brother Peter, supported her story and dismissed *The Star's* allegations as "fantasy." Even today, Peter Lee still believes that the scandal which enveloped his brother's death stemmed from the Hong Kong press' desire for revenge against Lee's brusque and often contemptuous attitude towards cameramen and journalists. "I can tell you one thing," he said, "when Bruce came back to Hong Kong, he had lots of enemies in the newspaper world."

But the damage had been done. *The Star's* revelations, fuelled by Betty Ting's neighbour who informed reporters that Lee had been a regular weekly visitor to the apartment for months prior to his death, had opened a floodgate. And once the Chinese scandal sheets took up the scent there was no closing it.

Exactly why Lee's confidants attempted to conceal the whereabouts of his collapse is still a mystery. "I don't know if Raymond said it," says Andre Morgan. "If he said it, I don't know why he said it." But the motivations behind such a cover-up, both on a personal and a professional level, aren't hard to understand. Probably out of a loyal, but misguided, sense of face saving duty, Lee's closest friends unleashed a monster which was to haunt them for months to come. Together with the medical inability to determine cause of death, the evasions combined to cast Lee's final hours in a shadowy, sinister light. "He was an open man in life, but everything about him turned mysterious after his death," commented film director Li Hsiang-cheung.

On the eve of an impending hailstorm of dirty rumours and malicious gossip, Bruce Lee's symbolic funeral took place in Hong Kong on Wednesday July 25th. Just how much he had meant to the people of his homeland can be judged by the manner in which the city mourned its king, a scene equalled only by the death of Rudolph Valentino half a century before. Here is a contemporary newspaper account of Valentino's funeral taken from New York's *Daily Mirror* on August 24th, 1926: "In life Rudolph Valentino drew excited, romance-hungry crowds. In death he draws a mob. Rudy lay in his silver and bronze coffin, a $10,000 coffin with an unbreakable glass over his face. The crowd would not be patient and would not wait to see him. They crashed in through a plate glass window, carrying the police with an angry roar, falling, screaming hitting out with their fists, stepping on those in their way. Horses trampled some of them. Others fainted. From 75 to 100 were hurt. But nothing could keep them away. There went a girl in her stockinged feet, weeping hysterically soaked to the skin, her new hat a ruin. She was crying: 'I must see him! I must see him!'"

Hong Kong's farewell was not quite as unrestrained as New York's hysterical display. But it came close.

The Kowloon Funeral Home where Lee lay in an open bronze coffin was packed from the moment it opened at 9.00 a.m., an hour before the ceremony was due to begin. Inside the tiny chapel, 60ft by 40ft, the stifling midsummer air was thick with the narcotic odour of flowers, incense and sweat. A tight mass of mourners and photographers jostled together before a portrait of the dead man set on an altar surrounded by candles and flowers. Long strips of fine silk floated down from the walls and were lost in the crush. At the entrance were piled more than 500 floral tributes from all over the world. Beside a

Hong Kong is stunned by the announcement of Lee's death. Thousands line the streets to honour his symbolic burial parade and scores of spectators were injured ion the crush. Steel barriers were erected along the coffin's route to restrain the crowd.

The press force their way across the funeral parlour to take their last photograph of Bruce Lee. In death, as in life, Lee's most private moments were invaded by the glare of the flash bulb.

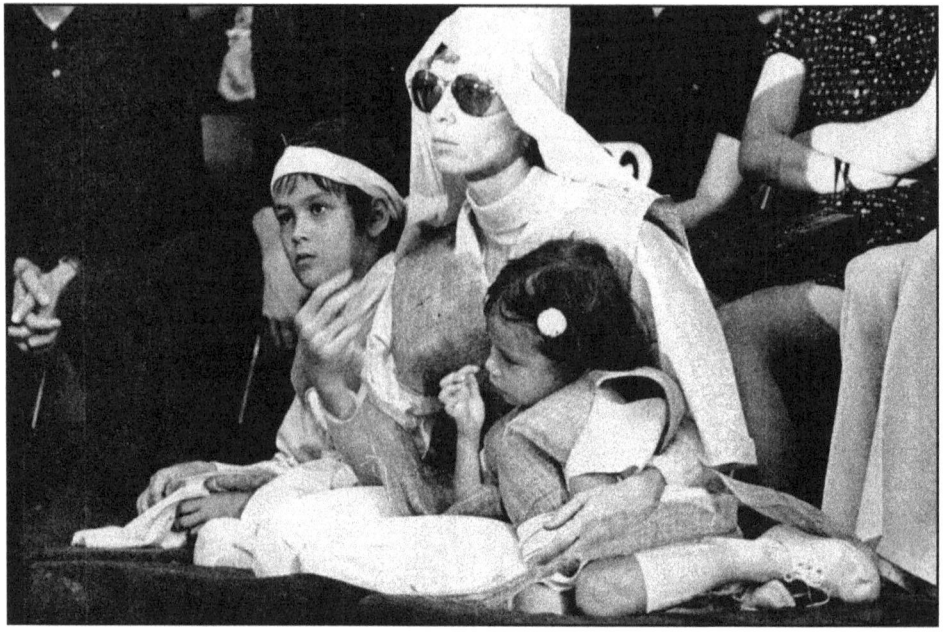

spray tearfully deposited by a six year old boy and carrying the simple message, "From a little fan," lay a wreath labelled, "To Bruce from Ting Pei". Lee's body, swathed to the chin in white silk, lay stiff and wooden in its bronze coffin, his face grey and distorted despite heavy make-up. A banner overhead proclaimed in Chinese: "A Star Sinks In A Sea Of Art."

Outside the funeral parlour, ten to twenty thousand distraught spectators lined the route of the funeral procession. Many had stood throughout the night behind steel barriers erected by the authorities. Others clambered precariously over the city's famous neon signs or perched on rooftops to catch a final glimpse of their idol's coffin. When they spotted celebrities making their way up the steps of the funeral home, they clapped and cheered. The *South China Morning Post* described the scene as "a carnival."

One after another the leading figures of the Mandarin film industry arrived: Nancy Kwan, who as Suzy Wong, had herself once focused international attention on her homeland; Nora Miao, Lee's long time co-star, already embroiled in the looming whirlpool of rumours; Madam To Sam-ku, an ageing figure from Bruce's child star career; George Lazenby, the man who had hoped to co-star with the James Bond of the Orient; pop singer Sammy Hui; and even director Lo Wei.

They came to walk the dozen steps to his coffin, bow low and pay their respects to a man who had whipped a flagging backyard industry into the hottest thing in world cinema. They were all there, with two glaring exceptions: an old man from the Shaw Brothers' empire, and the girl whose name was on everybody's lips. Perhaps she was already vaguely aware of the approaching agony. Perhaps she was a little afraid of those thousands of mourners. Perhaps she was simply too grief stricken to move. Whatever the reason, the day Hong Kong said its farewell to the man she had loved, Betty Ting Pei took a dose of sleeping pills and stayed at home in bed.

WHO KILLED BRUCE LEE

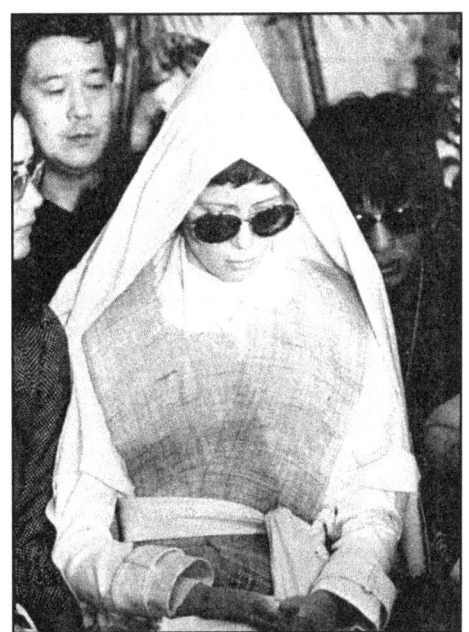

"For the scores of fans who had stayed up all night, the saddest moment was the arrival of Lee's wife Linda at about 9 a.m., reported the China Mail. For the 28-year-old American widow, her husband's funeral was a nightmare. Arriving with Raymond Chow and Golden Harvest production manager Ho Kun-cheung, she was greeted in silence by the five hundred mourners packed inside the funeral home. Almost lost in the heavy fold of her traditional white Chinese mourning gown, she presented an incongruous figure throughout the ancient ceremony. Red eyed behind dark glasses and flanked by her happily uncomprehending children, she sat cross legged on a cushion, an alien in a foreign land. The strain of waiting as wave after wave of friends and acquaintances took their turn before the coffin must have been almost unbearable, and she was reduced to tears many times. When the time came for her to make her own way to her husband's side, she look pitifully close to collapse. "It was a frightful time," she later confessed to her friends.

When the HK$40,000 coffin was carried from the funeral home, there was chaos, a grim replay of the opening scenes of *Fist of Fury* where Lee, as the student Chen, falls grief stricken on the coffin of his dead Kung Fu master. Three hundred policemen surrounding the parlour were forced to link arms and form a human chain to hold back the surging crowds. Eventually, reinforcements were called as women and children were repeatedly plucked clear of the barriers to prevent their being crushed. Old men wept, young girls fainted and many people were taken to hospital suffering from shock and minor injuries. "It was terrible alright," recalls Peter Lee.

If the behaviour of the Chinese fans seems at all bizarre, we must remember that they were mourning not simply the passing of a movie star, but the death of a man who had restored a lost pride in their heritage. The Chinese of Hong Kong had lost a Messiah, and they weren't about to give him up without a fitting display of emotion. Long after the

coffin was gone, police with loudspeakers were still patrolling the streets, urging people to return to their homes.

Lee was buried six days later at Seattle's Lake View Cemetery in a simple ceremony attended by one hundred and fifty friends and a hundred or so spectators. Among his pallbearers were Steve McQueen and James Coburn. "Farewell brother," said Coburn as Lee, dressed in the dark blue Chinese suit from *Fist of Fury*, was lowered into the earth. "As a friend and teacher you brought my physical, spiritual and psychological being together. Thank you and peace be with you." Looking considerably less shaken on her home territory, Linda told the gathering that she had tried to share in her husband's basic beliefs, "which he not only spoke but practiced in his daily life. He believed the individual represents the whole of mankind whether he lives in the Orient or elsewhere. He believed man struggles to find the life outside himself, not realising that the life he seeks is within him." She closed the service with a line from the Blood Sweat and Tears song, *When I Die*: "And when I'm dead, and when I'm gone, there'll be one child born in this world to carry on." Lee's grave was marked simply by flowers forming the Yin Yang symbol. Three months later, American fans were still flocking to the hill overlooking Lake Washington to pay their respect.

Back in Hong Kong, the news that Lee's bronze coffin had been damaged during the flight and had to be replaced in Seattle was greeted with much head-shaking by the old and wise of the Chinese community. "A bad omen," they muttered. "The soul of the buried man will not live in peace." They were not far wrong.

The press situation in Hong Kong is unique, something akin to a small aquarium tightly crammed with piranhas. Besides the colony's four English-language dailies, there are 101 Chinese papers, all fighting for a circulation totalling one and a quarter million readers. Naturally enough, the editorial climate is one of permanent throat-slitting competition, and out of this was born the notorious "Mosquito Press" - Hong Kong's sensationalist fly-by-night scandal sheets who "print with a sting." Sadly for Betty Ting Pei, *The Star*'s story had dropped her right in the middle of the man-eaters, and with still no official word on cause of death, it was not long after the last mourners had returned home that Bruce's superhero image was in there with her.

Michael Kaye: "You've got to remember that as far as the majority of Chinese people are concerned, a film actress is a whore and an actor is a stud. Any girl who is 'stacked' by Western standards - in other words she has a bosom you can palpably see - is a 'sexpot.' If you persuade her to act in films with sex scenes in them, she will very seldom undress herself; when it comes to the close-up of the breasts or hip or navel or whatever, it's usually a stand-in. But even so, she will get this reputation and gossip will condemn anybody in a place where moral standards are exactly those of America and Britain 70 years ago, where, without saying hypocrisy, everybody loves to be titillated but society is split into good girls and bad girls. Bad girls are actresses of any description, and poor old Betty was stuck with 'sexpot.'"

Within days of the funeral, the Mosquito Press was busy informing its credulous readers that Lee had died in Betty Ting Pei's apartment from an overdose of "707," a potent concoction which is the local equivalent of Spanish Fly. Besides "707," the Mosquitos also had Lee addicted to a whorehouse of drugs ranging from vitamin pills to LSD and heroin. From superhero, Lee suddenly became superstud, the lover of a dozen different women.

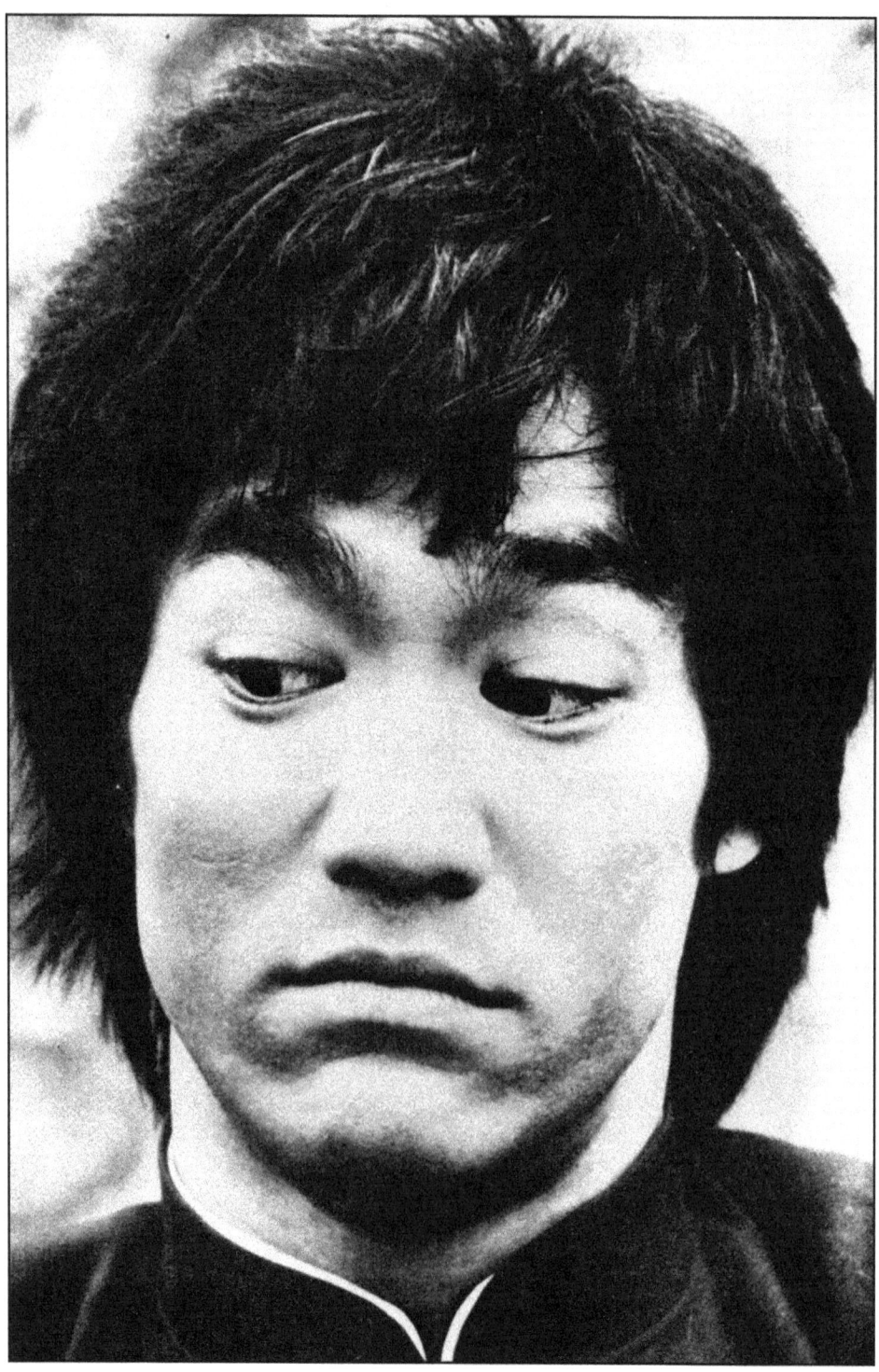

WHO KILLED BRUCE LEE

"The press decided they could add some spice to the story by not only including Betty Ting Pei, but all his other mistresses," says Andre Morgan. "What they did was to go back through all the files and get every photograph of him with a well known actress posing together. They had five pages of him with different chicks, you know. The arm around, smiling, the whole bit. The stories were rampant, stories about him dying from an overdose of drugs, dying from screwing too much, dying with an erection, dying from being hacked to death by young thugs, poisoned by his servant. There was one story that he wasn't really dead, that on the aeroplane, he woke up, got out of the coffin and when they got to Seattle, went down to the morgue and got another stiff, put it in the coffin and buried it in his place. I've really got him hiding in America - a big publicity stunt for bringing him back next year."

The luckless and unwilling star of this macabre circus was Betty Ting Pei. Branded a "scarlet woman" by the Mosquitos, she was blatantly implicated in Lee's death, and the public hung on every word. In Kuala Lumpur, students demonstrated carrying placards which read "Betty Killed Bruce." In Hong Kong, she was suspect number one and even today more Chinese than not will swear that Lee died from over-exertion that Friday night in Betty's bedroom.

There were attempts to check the storm cloud while it was still building. The day she left Hong Kong's Kai Tak airport with her husband's body, Linda issued a statement imploring the press and populace to end speculation on Lee's death. "Although we do not have the final autopsy report, I hold no suspicion of anything other than natural death," she said. "I myself do not hold any person or people responsible for his death. Fate has ways we cannot change. The only thing of importance is that Bruce is gone and will not return." A Golden Harvest spokesman added: "Now that a great star is dead, it's the wish of most film people to let him die like a hero. The reports, if true, will undoubtedly ruin his image. And they will break the heart of numerous Lee fans."

Betty Ting Pei went one step further and threatened to sue the press should they continue to publish the rumours. "It seems that people want me to die," she told *The Star*, "and if this continues, I just don't want to live on. Bruce is dead. Why don't you leave it at that?" But when one of the Mosquitos ran a front page headline challenging, "BETTY TING, SUE US!" over a fresh list of disclosures, the harassed girl fled into hiding. One of her close friends later confided: "She doesn't do much of anything except watch television."

Despite all the denials, pleas and threats, the rumour machine churned on. Multiplying each day, the gossip ensured that the Bruce Lee Death Drama remained front page news, week after week. Hong Kong could talk of little else.

Some of the stories seemed rooted in ground more solid than sensationalist copy. The Star, still smarting under the indignity of Lee's impending lawsuit (it was later dropped quietly by Linda), began an investigation into Lee's finances and turned up yet another headline allegation. When he died, Lee was virtually broke. According to *The Star*, 80% of his Concord holdings were registered in his butler's name - Wu Ngan, the boy Lee's father raised and with whom Bruce had grown up. Also, said The Star, Lee's Kowloon Tong home was owned by Lo Yuen Enterprises Ltd., one of the directors of which was Wu Ngan. When asked about his massive good fortune, Mr Wu said simply: "He trusted me" before retreating behind the locked gates of his house. *The Star* persisted in its investigation, and after checking with the local Rolls Royce agent, claimed that Lee's much heralded Rolls had nev-

WHO KILLED BRUCE LEE

er been ordered. Raymond Chow scoffed at the stories. "Bruce had enough money when he died," he said. "He could well afford a Rolls Royce and a house among other things."

Whatever the truth of *The Star* allegations, most of the rumours flying about Hong Kong were malicious fantasy. The product of a sensation-hungry press, foolishly fed half truths by second hand sources, they catered to a grieving readership in search of scapegoats. The search did not continue long. In early August, police were called to investigate a suspicious brown paper parcel bearing the Chinese label: "Betty Ting knows the cause of Bruce Lee's death." The bomb scares involving similar parcels with such messages as "Revenge for Bruce Lee." Finally, with no end in sight to the slander and allegations destroying more than a hapless Taiwanese actress, the Hong Kong government ordered a full scale official inquiry into the whole unhappy affair.

CHAPTER THREE

STICKS, STONES & BAD FENG SHUI

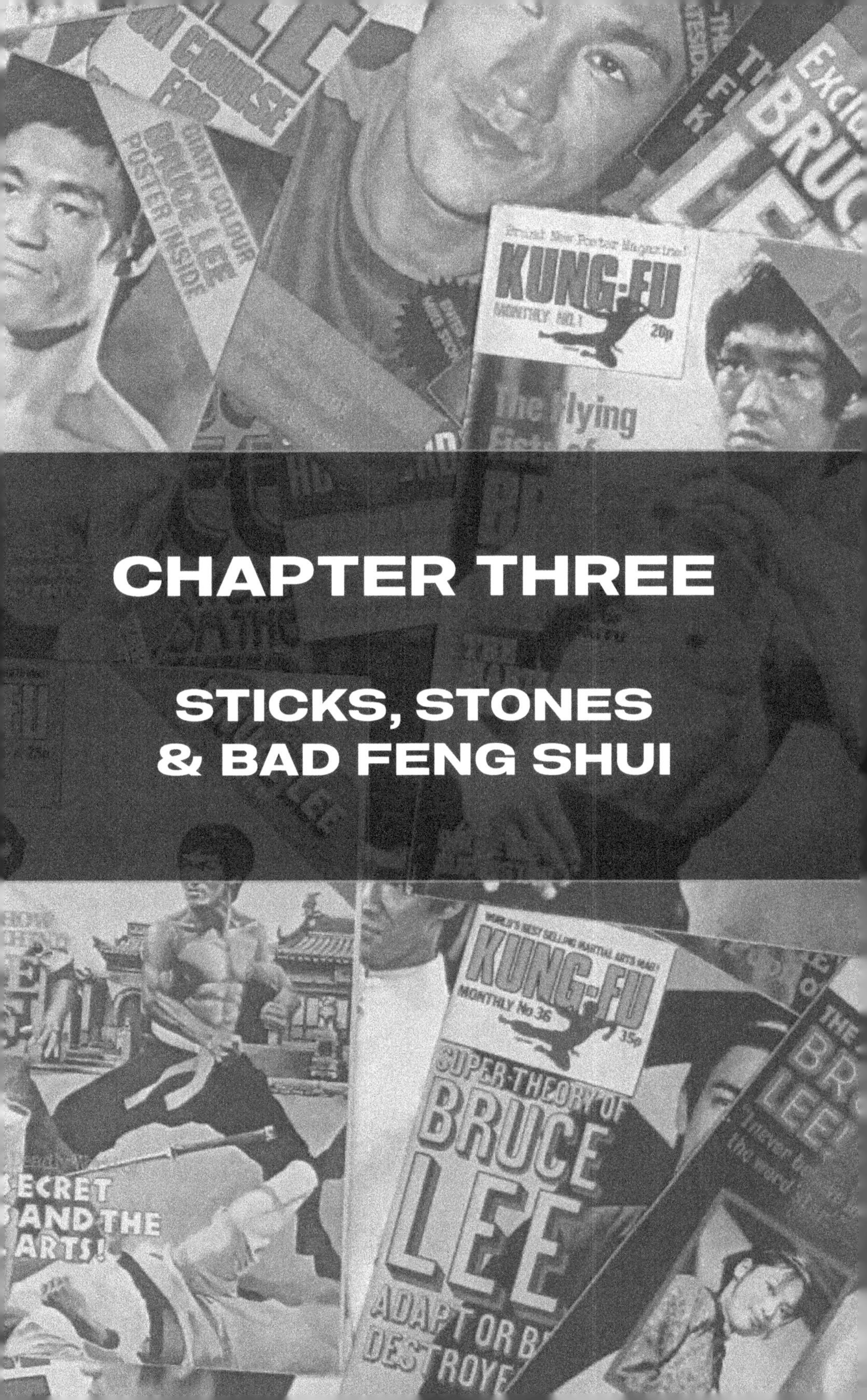

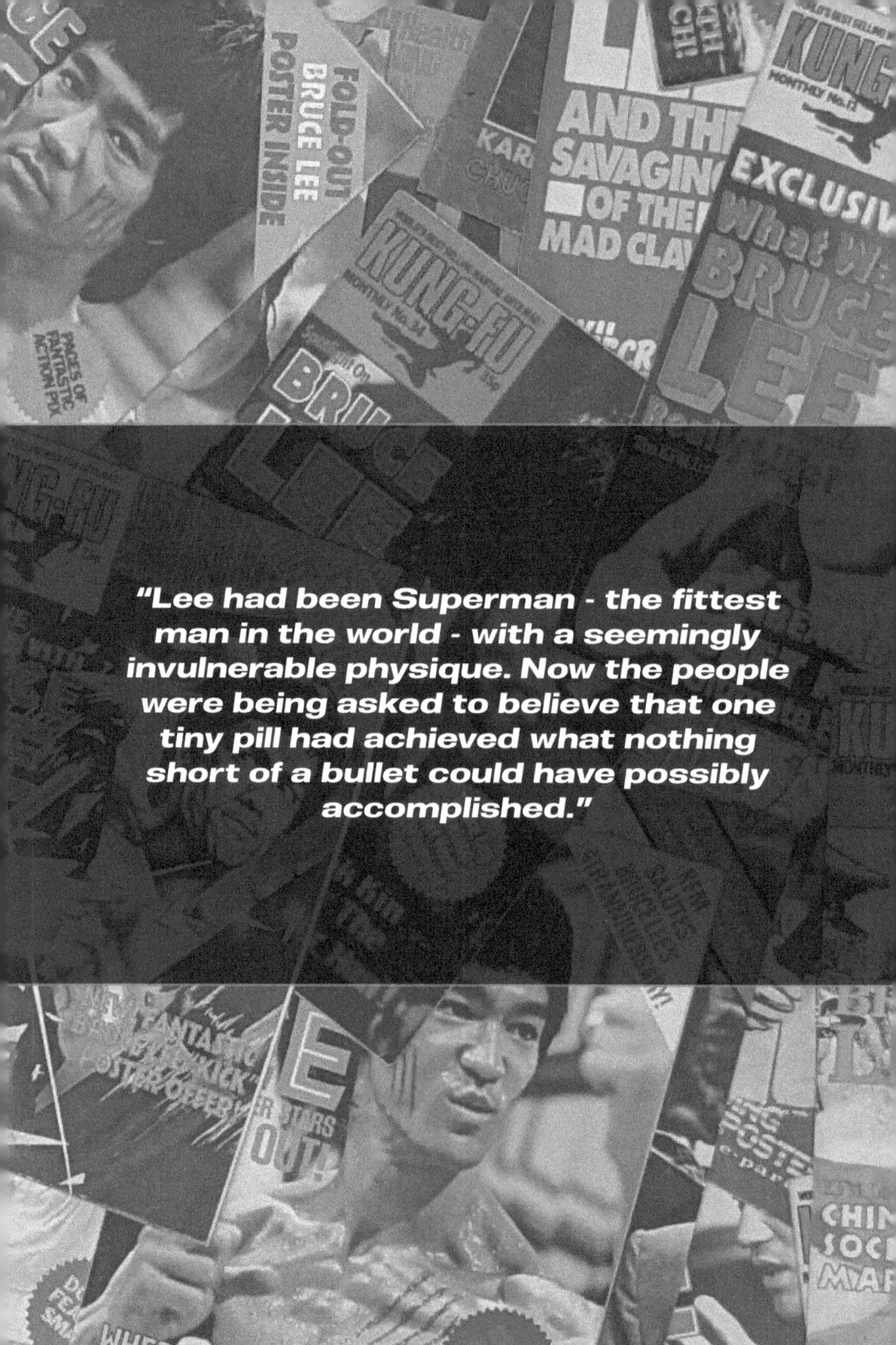

"Lee had been Superman - the fittest man in the world - with a seemingly invulnerable physique. Now the people were being asked to believe that one tiny pill had achieved what nothing short of a bullet could have possibly accomplished."

WHO KILLED BRUCE LEE

The inquest into Bruce Lee's death was an official attempt to stem once and for all the cesspool of malice and intrigue sweeping the colony. The Hong Kong government, itself embarrased by the ambulance officer's remarks to *The Star*, (an inter-departmental memo was circulated after that incident warning civil servants against talking to the press), spared no expense in securing evidence. The authorities hoped that under the public scrutiny afforded by an open inquiry, the truth would surface and speculation cease. After twenty-one days of thorough investigation, the court had before it, the "true story" according to Lee's friends, colleagues and relatives, pages of medical opinion and a definitive verdict. That the rumours continued unabated to this day can be viewed as an indication of how deeply Lee's death mystery has become entrenched in the minds of the people of Hong Kong. Years later Lee's demise still hangs over the colony like an apparition.

On September 3rd 1973, the inquest opened at Tsunwan before Coroner Egbert Tung. From the outset it proved to be a newspaper editor's dream. Crowds anxious to hear Betty Ting Pei's version of events, packed the spectators' gallery and over-flowed down the courthouse steps in their hundreds. Finally the police erected steel barriers to dampen the noisy enthusiasm. Inside, Mr. Tung was busy compiling the first complete and accurate account of Lee's last hours which, pieced together from the testimony of the various key witnesses who saw him that night, runs as follows:

> Linda Lee: *I saw him on July 20th at home. I left the house myself at about 12.30 p.m. and I left my husband at home.*
> Joe Duffy (Crown Counsel): *How was he then?*
> Linda: *He was fine.*
> Duffy: *Was he in a happy state?*
> Linda: *At that time he was.*
> Duffy: *Did you know his plan?*
> Linda: *Vaguely. He said he was meeting Raymond Chow to discuss a new film and that he would probably have dinner later on and would not be coming home to dinner.*

At approximately 2 p.m. Chow called at Lee's Cumberland Road home where the two men discussed the extensively rewritten *Game of Death* script before leaving for Betty Ting Pei's apartment to offer her a part in the film. They arrived at about 4 p.m. and talked for several hours over soft drinks before Lee complained of a headache. Betty Ting Pei gave him a prescription pain killing tablet called Equagesic and shortly after he went to bed. At 7.30 p.m. Chow left the apartment to keep a dinner appointment with George Lazenby at the Miramer Hotel. Lee was to follow on later.

> Chow: *Mr Lee said that he would see me in the restaurant and then went to the bedroom. I went to the washroom and after that I left.*
> Duffy: *The tablet that he had taken, at what time did he take it?*
> Chow: *I would say about half an hour after he complained of a headache.*
> Duffy: *Where there any symptoms other than a headache?*
> Chow: *Not that I could see.*

Duffy: *Apart from the tablet that he took, did you see him taking anything else?*
Chow: *No.*

During the course of the evening after Chow had departed, Betty Ting Pei attempted twice to wake the sleeping Lee but failed to provoke any response. Eventually she telephoned Raymond Chow who returned to the apartment at approximately 9.30 p.m. Lee appeared to be "sleeping soundly," but even slaps to the face could not bring him to. Betty Ting Pei then telephoned her personal physician, Dr. Chu Phohwye, who examined Lee and immediately called for an ambulance to take him to the Queen Elizabeth Hospital. Chow returned to Cumberland Road to escort Linda to the hospital.

The press in Hong Kong the day after Lee's death had quoted Raymond Chow as saying that when Lee failed to arrive for the dinner engagement with Lazenby, he had telephoned the Cumberland Road house and learned that Lee was ill. No mention of Betty Ting Pei or her Beaconsfield Road apartment had been leaked to the press. "I rushed around to his home and it was decided he should go to hospital," said Chow according to *The Star*. When Chow denied at the inquest telling the press on July 21st he had seen Lee at Cumberland Road, there were boos from the packed press benches.

The next bombshell to rock Tsunwan came on September 17th when Bruce's wife, Linda Lee took the stand and confirmed a story widely circulated after Lee's autopsy that her husband had taken cannabis. Surprisingly, in a colony which in 1973 recorded the seizure of 1,748 kilos of opium, 399 kilos of morphine and 50 kilos of heroin, cannabis is still regarded by the Hong Kong police, press and public as a major evil. When cannabis traces had been discovered in Lee's stomach and small intestine during the autopsy, his death was openly attributed to an "overdose" of the drug. "BRUCE TOOK CANNABIS

- LINDA!" trumpeted the afternoon papers following Linda's testimony and for several days the inquest was plunged into a debate on the lethal capabilities of cannabis.

After the May 10th collapse, Linda told Coroner Tung, her husband had admitted to Dr. Wu of St. Theresa's Hospital that he had taken cannabis that same day.

> Duffy: *Did you hear Dr. Wu warn him against it?*
> Linda: *He said it was harmful. Subsequently, we went to the U.S. to discuss cannabis with a neurologist and have a check-up. The neurologist said that moderate doses were not harmful. The doctors denied the fact that cannabis had anything to do with the collapse (of May 20th).*

Linda asserted that following the first collapse, Lee had taken cannabis "only occasionally" and that there had been no after-effects. In reply to Mr. David Yapp, (representing the American International Assurance Company), she said Lee had told her that March or April was the first time he had tried the drug. Because of his professional need to keep fit, she added, "he would not be so foolish to use cannabis more than just occasionally."

The cannabis controversy drew to a close when government chemist Dr. Ronald Lam testified that New Zealand laboratory tests together with his own examinations had found only minute amounts of cannabis in Lee's stomach and intestine. And after Professor Ronald Teare of London University's Foren-

THE KUNG-FU MONTHLY ARCHIVE SERIES

sic Medicine Department (who had flown to Hong Kong specifically to give evidence), argued that he considered the cannabis found in Lee's body "about as significant as if I had been told Lee had taken a cup of tea or coffee," the issue fizzled out altogher, except for the insistent questioning of Mr. Yapp. An escape clause in the AIAC insurance policy on Lee's life (variously estimated by the press at between HK$500,000 and HK$2,000,000), signed on January 19th 1973, allowed the company to withhold payment if it was proven that Lee had used narcotics prior to that date. Mr. Yapp therefore persistently quizzed medical witnesses about the effects of cannabis and their views on the drug. After the inquest had closed, there were press reports that AIAC had hired a private detective to investigate Lee's drug experiences. The Hong Kong police also probed Lee's drug connections, but after questioning several well known names in the film industry they quietly closed their files.

As soon as the cannabis saga had run its course, the inquest reverted to a more complex medical analysis of the various prescription drugs Lee had been taking. Although the media continued to report proceedings each day for an audience thirsting after explosive revelations, the courtroom drama became something of a dreary non-event. After Betty Ting Pei had come briefly out of hiding, presented her unspectacular evidence and had been discharged, the public lost interest altogether and the steel barriers were removed from Tsunwan.

In essence, the dozens of pages of medical evidence determined that Lee had regularly used two prescription drugs: a pain killer, Doloxene, which had been prescribed after he had injured his back in 1968, and the epilepsy control drug, Dilantin, prescribed by Dr. Reisbord following the May 10th collapse. The tablet Equagesic which Betty Ting Pei

had given Lee on the night of his death, was analysed as a compound of aspirin and the drug meprobanate. Testimony was given that Equagesic, a tranquiliser available only on prescription, could prove dangerous if taken with alcohol. Dr. Lam told the court that he had searched for signs of other drugs in Lee's body - especially Spanish Fly - but had found no traces.

Dr. R. R. Lycette of the Queen Elizabeth Hospital suggested that hypersensitivity to Equagesic or Doloxene had triggered the seizure, causing Lee's brain to swell from a normal weight of 1,400 grammes to 1,575 grammes. "The brain was swollen like a spong," he said. Professor Teare, who in his 35-year career had performed 90,000 postmortems and given evidence before 18,000 inquests, supported Dr. Lycette's theory. Lee, he declared, had died from "acute cerebral oedema, (brain swelling), due to the hypersensitivity to either meprobanate or aspirin or a combination of the two found in Equagesic." "Hypersensitivity in this case is very rare indeed," he added. Rare, perhaps, but lethal enough to kill a man at the peak of his physical development?

On September 24th, following a brief discussion on the technical differences between the words "accident" and "misadventure," Mr. Egbert Tung delivered a verdict of "death by misadventure." The court and the authorities were satisfied with Professor Teare's argument. The people of Hong Kong were not.

Following the sudden and unexpected death of any popular celebrity, there is inevitably rumour and speculation. Consider this article from the *New York Daily News* of April 24th, 1926, which threw the city into a morbid panic.

There flew along Broadway yesterday sinister reports that Rudolph Valentino came to his death by arsenic poisoning. Circumstantial stories told of both jealousy and revenge as the supposed motives. Immediately upon the heels of the first report Dr. William B. Rawles of Polyclinic Hospital denied formally that he had been poisoned. When this story appeared, it spread through New York like wildfire. Even after it had been established that the News had invented the "sinister reports" to gain ground in a savage circulation war raging amongst the press of the time, the rumours persisted for many months. Times change but human nature is immutable; admirers at any place or at any time can scarcely resist the temptation to make jigsaw puzzles out of the private lives of their fallen idols.

Bruce Lee, as a world class movie star and a virtual messiah in his own country, could hardly have escaped this myth creating process had he passed away from entirely natural causes in the presence of a dozen high court judges. As it was, a score of official inquests could not have squashed Oriental speculation over his death. There had been too many cover-ups, too many half-truths and whitewashed relationships, too many shadows and rattling skeletons for the citizens of Hong Kong to happily accept a simple explanation. In addition, Lee had been Superman, "the fittest man in the world" with a seemingly invulnerable physique. Now the people were being asked to believe that one tiny pill had achieved what nothing short of a bullet could have possibly accomplished. Like a flow of dirty lava, the foul play and conspiracy theories snowballed long after Mr. Tung had packed his wig and moved on to other corpses. The key figure was, and to this day still is, Betty Ting Pei. According to the most popular rendition of their relationship, Lee met Betty a year before his death and they became extremely close. At one point, so rumour has it, Lee attempted to end the affair, resuming it only after Betty had broken down and been admitted to hospital. Friends of Ting Pei with whom I spoke in Hong Kong openly confirmed that there was a romantic liaison between Bruce and Betty. Linda Lee, Golden Harvest and other acquaintances of Bruce however, deny any deep involvement. "If he was having an affair with her then he was doing a good job of keeping it secret," says An-

WHO KILLED BRUCE LEE

dre Morgan. "I know a lot of things are being said now that make him seem that he wasn't always as beautiful as I think he was," said Linda on Radio Hong Kong, "but so much of what is said you must not believe because it's rumour and it's absolutely untrue. He was just a human being, he wasn't perfect, but he was a very, very beautiful person inside. He was always very good to me. I could not have a complaint in the world. I could not wish for a better husband ever."

Whatever the truth of Lee's private life, many of the Chinese of Hong Kong have tried Lee and reached their own verdict. Or, rather, they have accepted the trial and judgement of the mosquito press. While on a recent trip to Taiwan, journalist Peter Bennett caught a taxi and during the ride, steered the conversation around to Lee's death. "Ay yes," nodded the cab driver knowingly, "too much sex..." which in a nutshell sums up much current popular Eastern sentiment. Under scrutiny, the theory is as leaky as the hulk of the Queen Elizabeth which lies rusting at the bottom of Hong Kong harbour, but to the Chinese it is the popular gospel according to the mosquitos. "The original founder starts off with hypotheses, but then they become gospel truth," Lee once described as the principle behind the freedoms of Jeet Kune Do. Little did he realise he was voicing his own epitaph.

With the Bruce Lee cult now in full sway around the world, speculation on his death has spread to the West. Andre Morgan: "I had a letter from Canada the other day, from Goose Bay, Labrador - some weird place where I never would have thought they'd heard of Bruce Lee. A lady writes in - a housewife with three children - saying she and her family had just seen one of Bruce's movies and they understood that he was dead and could we please confirm the story that the Mafia had shot him because he was getting too big and they couldn't control him anymore. There are all sorts of weird stories floating around, all

THE KUNG-FU MONTHLY ARCHIVE SERIES

WHO KILLED BRUCE LEE

 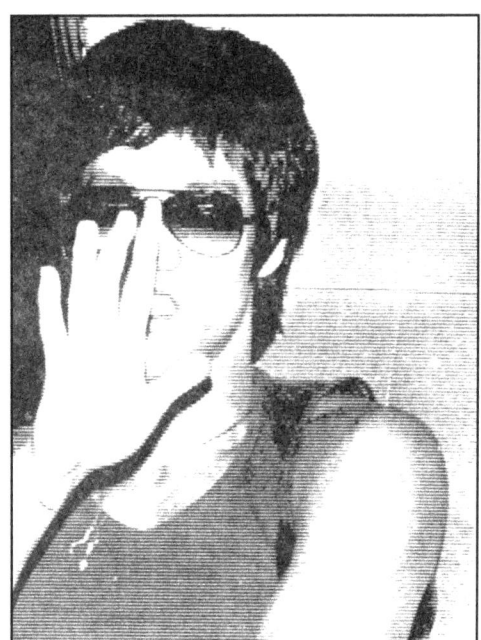

over creation."

In a book recently published in the U.S., *The Legend of Bruce Lee* (Dell Books), author Ben Block quotes Los Angeles Karate instructor Ed Parker as saying he considers "foul play" was involved. Parker, according to Block, believes Lee may have been given a drug that would not have shown up at the autopsy performed 36 hours after his death. "Many of us do not know the inner thinking and secrets of those herbalists in China," Parker is quoted as saying. "They have herbs for medicine and they have ones we've never heard of for poison. I believe it was foul play, but I don't think we will ever know for sure." Parker declines to even guess at who might have been behind this "foul play".

Author Block himself indulges in some speculation on Lee's death, suggesting Lee may have been "done in" buy a martial artist angered at his extravagant lifestyle, his championing of Jeet Kune Do at the expense of traditional styles, or by his publicising and exploitation of the hidden secrets of Kung-Fu. Perhaps, writes Block, a Shaolin monk or a Ninja (a member of the ancient assassination society) sought revenge on Lee. Or maybe Lee was killed by a "delayed death strike" administered by a practioner of the little known "art of the vibrating palm," the exponents of which can apparently convert their internal energy into vibrations, lay their palm on a victim and kill him at a pre-determined hour, be it two months or ten years from the time of contact.

At best, these theories sound fantastic, and Block himself seems highly sceptical, though certainly Lee had more than his fair share of enemies. Lee was the man with the golden punch, the martial Midas touch, and success had dogged him to his very grave. But as in any competition, be it business or sport, success is a provocative and often dangerous tag to bear. And to aggravate matters, Lee was by no means the easiest of competitors. On and off the set, in and out of the gymnasium, Lee destroyed face like a leprous aftershave. Winning, for him, was the prime goal. Even his own fighting technique, the conglomeration of styles that makes up Jeet Kune Do, aims solely at the swiftest way to superiority over an opponent. And where there is a winner, there must also be a loser. To many of those beaten by Lee in business or in the ring, his supreme self-confidence was unbearable, his blunt candidness an insult. Then again, Lee cost many of his rivals large amounts of money. Besides siphoning off much audience support from the established studios, there were numerous complaints that, under competition from the Lee films, smaller production companies foundered and were squeezed out of the race.

Lee irrevocably altered not only the products of the Mandarin film industry, but also the structure of the industry itself. As the first Mandarin actor to take control over his own career, he showed the way to a more equitable share of the profits for his fellow performers. Certainly in Hong Kong in the early months of 1973 there were many people who would have been more than happy to ring down the final curtain on the meteoric rise of Lee's star; but a Ninja in Kowloon Tong? Maybe...

Other Western wonderings on Lee's demise were voiced by folk singer Phil Ochs in the 15th February 1974 edition of London's *Time Out* magazine: "There were rumours in Hollywood of cocaine. Maybe he was killed by some crazy person or some rival business faction. Maybe he lived more intensely than any human being can live. Or maybe he died for the same reason James Dean died. They had taken too much of the fire and the gods were jealous." Maybe...

As the West ponders, the old and wise of Hong Kong's Chinese community are certain they hold the key to Lee's death. The fortune tellers of that city have compiled a list of omens which they firmly believe could only have resulted in fatality. Before you scoff, let us add that the fortune tellers warned him of his peril and that Lee, a believer in omens, took careful notice.

Feng Shui, (fortune telling), is an unbending law governing the lives of Hong Kong's four million Chinese. Even trivial day to day decisions are influenced by the Feng Shui experts' predictions and opinions: a businessman negotiating a contract will seek guidance, a family contemplating moving house will ask advice on the new location. According to experts, Lee's move to Kowloon Tong was a fatal error. For centuries, Kowloon Tong (literally "Nine Dragon Pond") has been the home of nine dragons and when Lee took up residence in the suburb, it caused anger and rivalry amongst those mythical beasts. As Lee was only a "Little Dragon," he was killed.

There were other Feng Shui omens heralding Lee's demise. One of the reasons that Kowloon Tong is shunned by Chinese residents is its reputation as a destroyer of rich families. Lee's Cumberland Road house in particular is regarded as a vicious financial equaliser. Situated at the lowest point of a natural depression (the "Dragon Pond"), it cannot apparently be lavishly decorated without provoking bad Feng Shui. Three years ago, a Chiuchow wig merchant bought the house from a Chinese widow for HK$400,000, and as it was in a ramshackle condition, he spent a further HK$300,000 on restoration work. Five months later the merchant, went bankrupt and was forced to sell the house to another wig merchant - an American - at a loss of HK$100,000. Soon after, he too suffered a severe business setback and fell seriously ill. In December of 1972, Bruce Lee purchased the ill-fated house through an agent for an estimated HK$1,000,000 and as soon as he moved in, Feng Shui began playing tricks. Every member of the Lee household fell ill in rotation, including the family dog. On the advice of friends, Lee installed a bad Feng Shui reflector - a small mirror set in an octagonal wooden frame known as a "Pa Kua" - on his roof. On July 18th, one of the region's frequent and devastating typhoons struck Hong Kong, blowing down a tree in Lee's back yard - itself a bad omen - and carrying away the reflector. Before Lee could replace it, he was dead.

A more obvious prophecy was read into the title of Lee's final film, *Game of Death*. It was reported that Golden Harvest director Lo Wei, remembering a top Chinese actor who had died in a car crash ten years previously after filming the movie titled *Rendezvous with Death*, warned that the film was tempting fate. Even poor Betty Ting Pei was herself seen as another bad omen. The *I Ching* teaches that all things in the universe are composed of five elements: gold, wood, water, fire and earth. These five elements have the capability of either helping or harming each other, depending on their relative harmony. In Chinese, the name of the road where Lee lived and Betty Ting Pei's name both belong to the element gold. Lee's name belonged to the element wood. According to the *I Ching*, gold is harmful to wood.

Bad Feng Shui, nine dragons, typhoons, film titles, warring elements; maybe these are

behind the untimely death of Bruce Lee. Maybe...

If there is room for speculation, perhaps a more legitimate focal point might be found in Lee's own fanatically nurtured body. After the Golden Havest collapse on May 10th, doctors then detected brain swelling and yet Lee had not taken Equagesic. Epilepsy was discussed and yet at his check up in the U.S., a board of medical experts could diagnose no disease or physical impairments; they told him in fact that he had the body of an 18-year-old. Less than two months later, following a period of startling and inexplicable weight loss, Lee was dead. Were these two events merely an extraordinary coincidence?

When Lee's mother-in-law learned of his death in Seattle, she immediately diagnosed the cause as "overwork." Certainly the reason is more complex than that, but perhaps she was not so far from the truth. In the months leading up to his death, Bruce Lee was working harder than he had ever worked. Starting with the *The Big Boss*, he made movies back to back - acting, writing, directing, dubbing and dealing for two years. "He was feeling very tired prior to his death for a couple of months," says Andre Morgan. "He'd been

WHO KILLED BRUCE LEE

working very hard and was under tremendous pressure. We'd finished *Enter the Dragon* and had dubbed it; we were getting ready for the big release in the fall as Warners had picked it as their big picture." Not that four films in two years is a heavy schedule by Hong Kong standards. There are actors and actresses in the colony who number their films in the hundreds, and it is not uncommon for a performer to work on more than one film at a time. But Bruce Lee was no ordinary performer.

The word used most frequently to describe Lee in martial arts movie circles is undoubtedly "perfectionist." Nothing that Lee started was allowed to fall below his own standards; if it did, he would fly into a rage and storm around the set or studio shouting to himself in English: "What should I do?" Andre Morgan: "He could be very annoying, he wanted things to be just right. For example, he spent a whole morning doing one fight sequence, something like a dozen takes. We viewed the rushes; the third, fourth and fifth takes were all good and yet he had gone on and done the sixth, seventh, eighth and so on because at the time he didn't feel comfortable about them." When rehearsing a fight scene including nunchakus, he would practice so hard that his arms and shoulders would become a mass of bruises. "I don't want to do anything half-way," he said shortly before his death. "It has to be perfect."

It had to be perfect because Lee's philosophy and ambition would settle for nothing less. The same ambition that had pushed Lee to the pinnacle of the martial arts pile, drove him at a crazy pace on a wild, dazzling trip through the film world of two continents. In search of perfection, Lee found himself at the very edge of a precipice.

Added to his work overload was the constant burden of living out a legend, holding together an impossible public image of racial saviour and "Fastest Fist in the East." The strain, to a man in love with his own superhuman image and yet shot through with the frailties of any human being, must have been close to intolerable; witness his temper outbursts at the press or his childish legal action against *The Star*.

"As a person he was very intense, deeply in everything," says Andre Morgan. "That was part of the problem, he was always going in too many directions at once to find out about everything as quickly as possible. He was always in a hurry." The May 10th collapse in the dubbing studio of Golden Harvest may have been a warning from a superbly honed but impossibly overtaxed body. If it was, Lee did not heed it. Two months later, he was a walking time bomb, trailing a fuse a mile long. All it needed was a spark; maybe that spark was a tablet marked Equagesic. Maybe...

THE KUNG-FU MONTHLY ARCHIVE SERIES

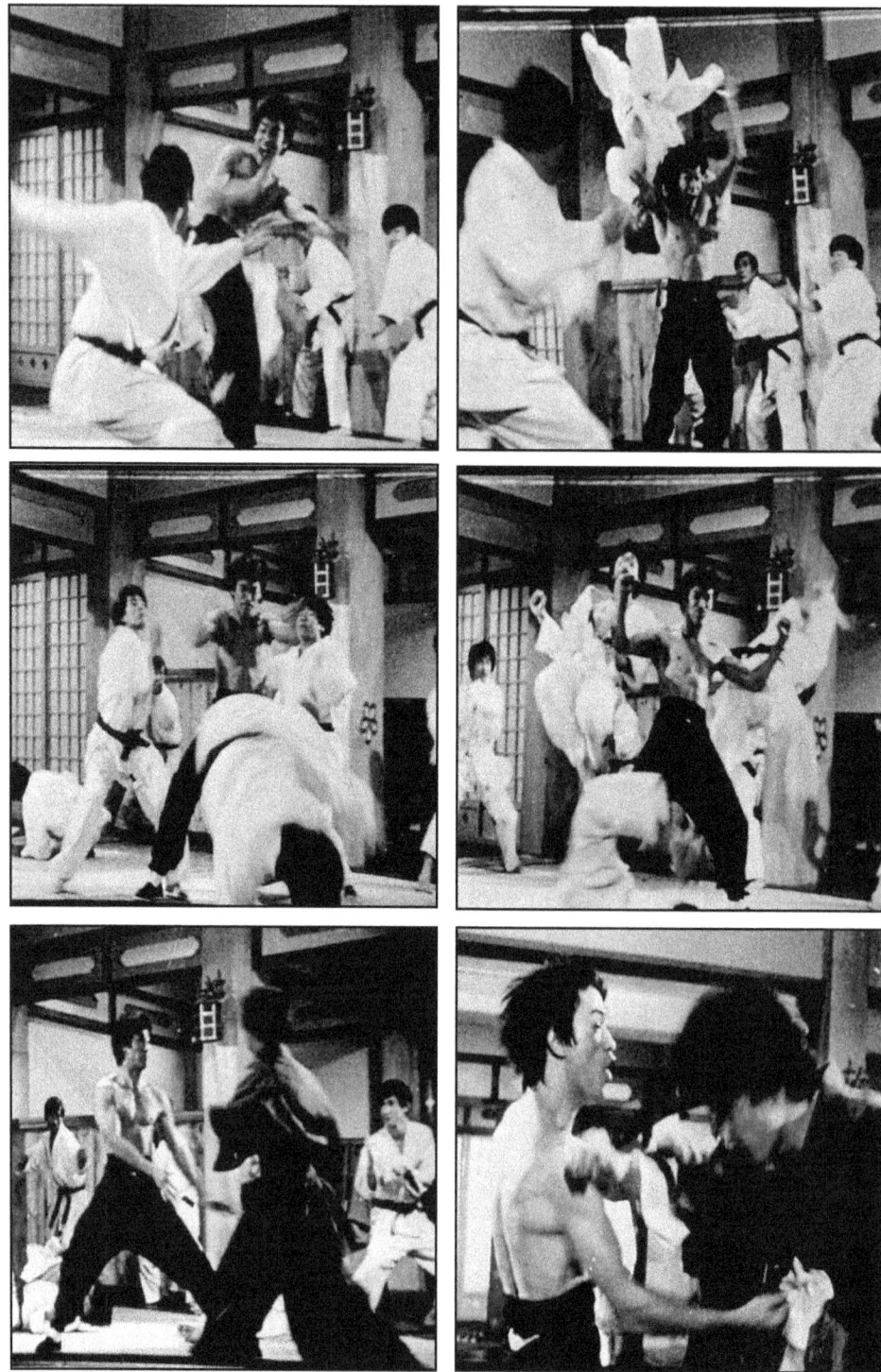

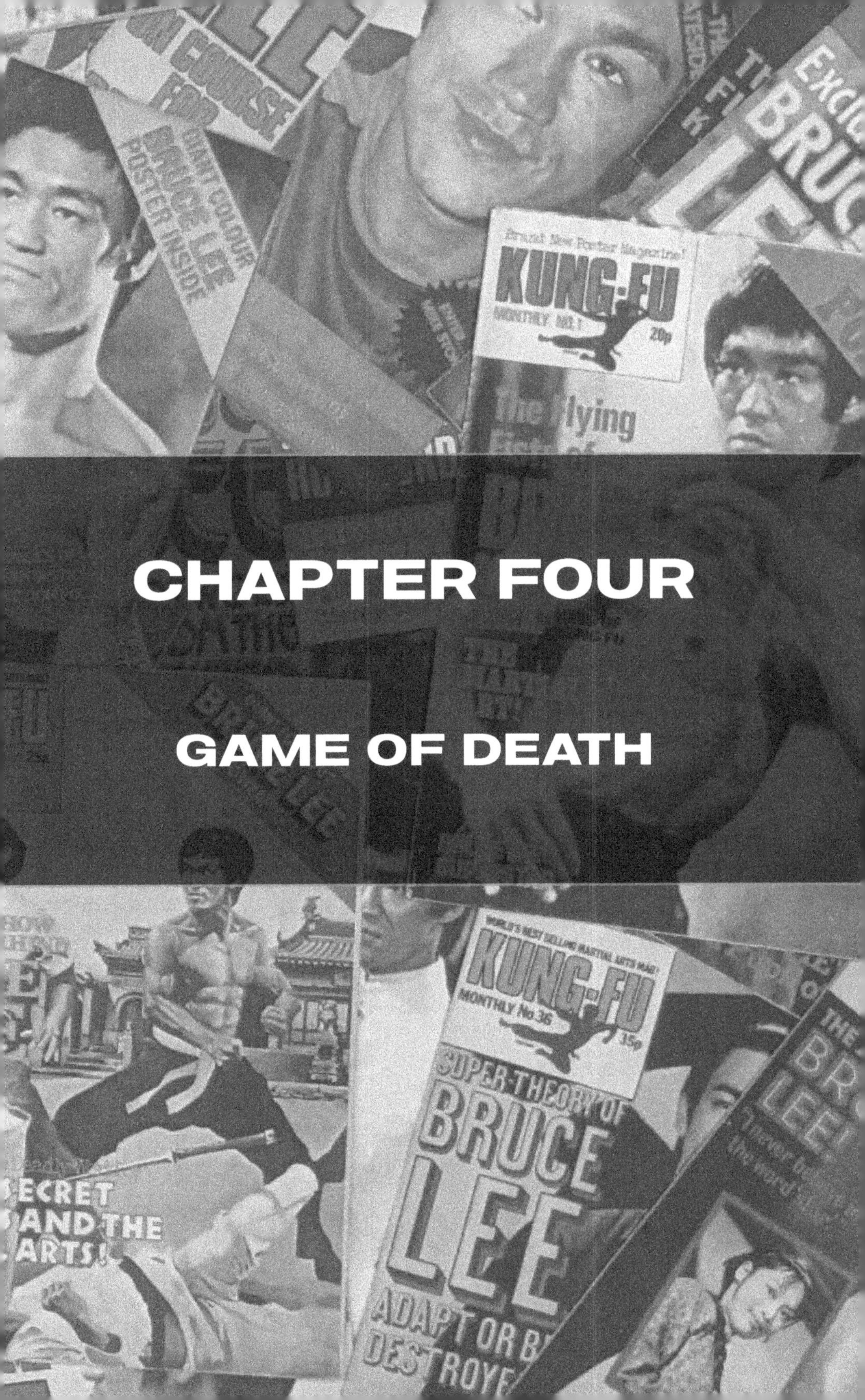

CHAPTER FOUR

GAME OF DEATH

"His movie-making is like his fighting. He just did it. He didn't know until the night before exactly what he was going to do. Then he put it together. He made up the story details as he went along, spontaneously. That's the way Game of Death was."

It has now been seven years since that fateful mid-July night in Hong Kong that Bruce Lee - the man they called the "Little Dragon" - died. In the days preceding his death, Lee knew that, after a decade of struggle, he had finally won. In the last few years of his brief life, he had single-handedly transformed the face of the massive Far East film industry, sparked a martial arts craze which was to sweep the globe, and rocketed from bit parts in television serials to the role of highest-paid actor in the world. Lee's career had exploded far beyond his wildest dreams, and 1973 - the year of *Enter the Dragon*, *The Way of the Dragon* and *Game of Death* seemed destined to seal his remarkable success. Truly, if every death robbed anyone of something more than life, it robbed Bruce Lee!

But it is a curious quirk of human society that in death heroes often attain heights which they could never have achieved in life. As it was with Rudolph Valentino, James Dean and Marilyn Monroe, so too was it with Bruce Lee. With his death, Lee passed into legend, and in the three years since that tragic evening, this legend took root and grew unchecked in the minds of his countless fans and followers. Lee himself would undoubtedly have been embarrassed and uneasy at the adulation which is now heaped upon him by his adoring fans. "Look, I'm the same guy I've always been," he once scolded one of his friends who had grown shy of approaching such a famous film star.

But as with Dean and Monroe, the Bruce Lee cult refused to die. Today, so long as his films continue their endless repeats in cinemas across five continents, the Little Dragon's fans will line the pavements. As long as Kung-Fu is practiced and mastered, his name will be remembered. It is this worship which has made Bruce Lee's last, unfinished, action epic - the eerily titled *Game of Death* - the most eagerly awaited film in cinema history! And, perhaps the most mysterious!

For three years, the footage Bruce Lee managed to shoot for *Game of Death* has lain untouched in the vaults of Golden Harvest, the Hong Kong production company Lee helped build from a mere idea into the second largest studio in the East. Until now, only the barest details about *Game of Death* have leaked from Golden Harvest. "He was an open man in life, but everything about him turned mysterious after his death," commented a Hong Kong film director at Bruce's funeral, pin-pointing the impending controversy which would later surround Lee's last hours. This same comment could just as well apply to *Game of Death*. Under Lee's own direction, it was the most open of films, shot with the voluntary assistance of a score of Lee's friends and acquaintances. After his death, the film became an enigma, caught up in the intrigue of the man's private life.

Now the news from Hong Kong is that *Game of Death* is back in production and tentatively scheduled for release later this year. Although officially the wraps are still on tight, enough detail has leaked out for an accurate picture to be pieced together. This then, is the story behind probably the last great Kung-Fu movie ever - *Game of Death*!

Game of Death was born at the precise moment Bruce Lee's career began to erupt internationally. To producers in Hong Kong, the name Bruce Lee on the marquee was already a gilt-edged guarantee of at least a million dollars. Lee's first two films - *The Big Boss* and *Fist of Fury* (titled respectively *Fists of Fury* and *The Chinese Connection* in the U.S.) - had shattered box office records throughout the Far East and reaped extraordinary profits for Golden Harvest. So great was Lee's impact on the Eastern Industry that the Chinese producers began thinking seriously for the first time ever of exporting their wares to

the West. Kung Fu, it was felt, might just take off.

The first producer to take the plunge was Run Run Shaw, head of the giant Shaw Brothers Studios and acknowledged czar of Oriental film-making. His *King Boxer* (*Five Fingers of Death* in the U.S.) starring Lo Lieh, was the Westerners' first taste of Kung Fu and it was immediately obvious that a Kung Fu invasion was imminent. In just eleven weeks, *Five Fingers* notched up a cool $3,800,000 in the U.S. alone!

After several other Shaw Bros. movies had been released in the West, Golden Harvest decided to launch Bruce Lee's first effort, *The Big Boss*. Standing head and shoulders above any other actor in the East, Lee's appeal was a foregone conclusion. Overnight, the Western fans transformed him into an international superstar!

At this time, Lee had already completed his third film - *The Way of the Dragon* (*Return of the Dragon* in the U.S.). *The Way of the Dragon* was Bruce's first solo film-making effort. Besides playing the leading role, he had elbowed out veteran director Lo Wei and taken control himself, working from his own script. Perhaps more importantly, he had technically 'left' Golden Harvest and had set up his own film company - Concord - together with Raymond Chow, the Big Boss of Golden Harvest. The move meant not only that Lee would receive a cut in the profits from his films - an unheard of arrangement in the old fashioned Hong Kong film world - but from now on, he would have complete say in what he was doing. Lee's ambition, so often the driving force in his life, demanded that he pull the

strings. For the first time in his career, he was in a position to do just that. What he decided on was a film which he had vaguely planned in his mind, a film which would provide the ultimate showcase for the martial arts. For many months, his concept of the film was so sketchy that he did not even give it a working title. Later though, he would refer to it as *Game of Death*.

Lee began actual filming for *Game of Death* long before the ideas in his mind had congealed into anything even resembling a story line. He had originally planned to take a breather after *The Way of the Dragon* was complete, work out a plot, write a script, choose a cast and crew and then begin cranking the camera. However, this schedule was thrown into confusion by the appearance of a giant from Milwaukee - Kareem 'Big Lew' Abdul-Jabbar. Bruce and Kareem, an ace centre player for the Milwaukee Bucks and one of the top basketball players in America, had been friends for many years. When Bruce heard that he was planning a visit to Hong Kong, he wrote to him suggesting that they shoot some footage together for *Game of Death*. Perhaps his father's theatrical background helped Bruce see the showmanship possibilities in a Kung Fu bout between himself and a man a full two foot taller than him! Kareem readily agreed and shortly after his arrival, he visited the Golden Harvest studios and began work.

Although Jabbar could never claim to come within a mile of equalling Lee's martial

WHO KILLED BRUCE LEE

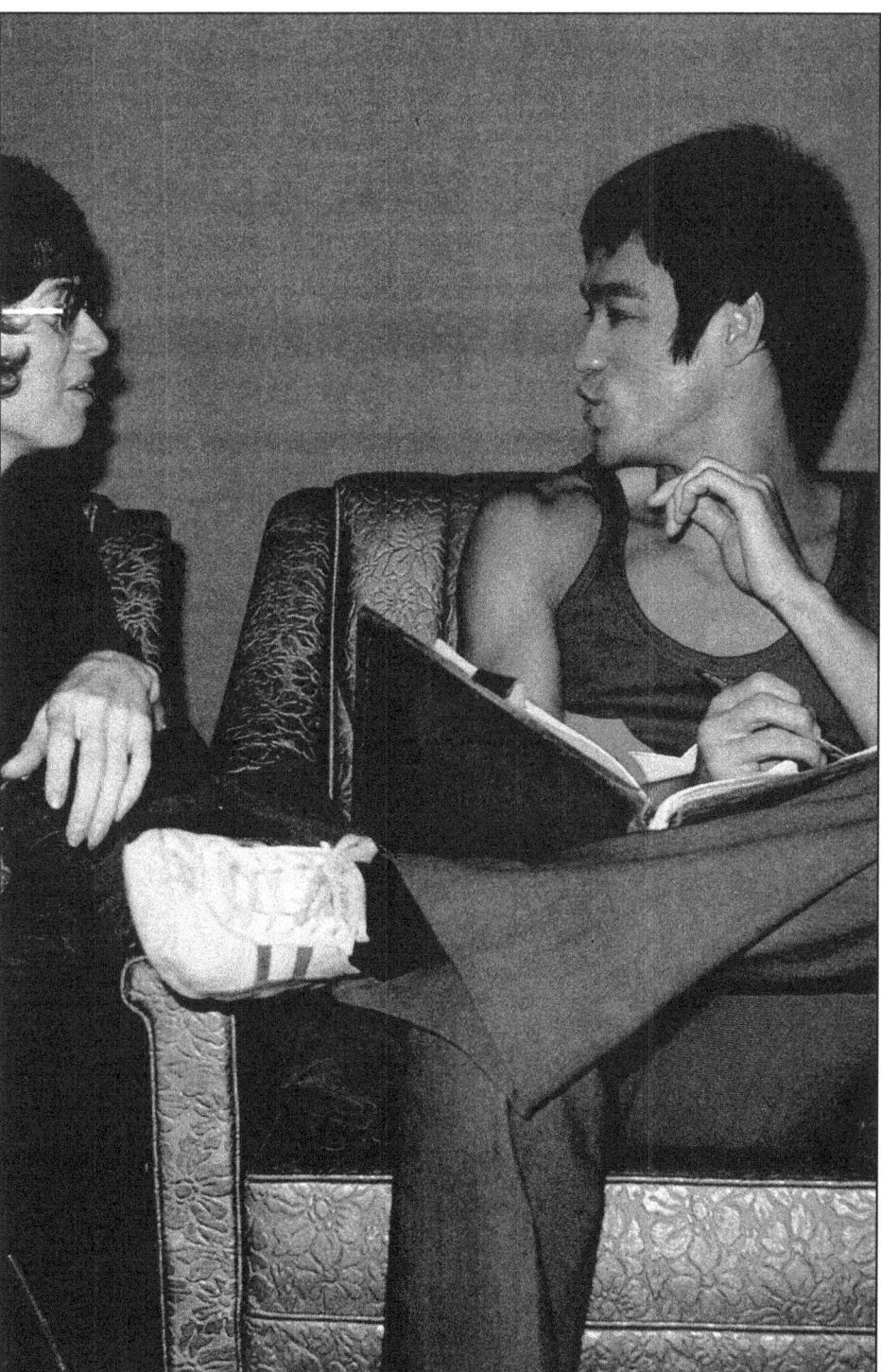

prowess, the scenes which unfolded were apparently highly realistic and entertaining, a masterly mixture of the sublime and the ridiculous. Shooting took a full week, and when it was complete, cast, crew and extras were all profoundly pleased. Everyone, that is, except Jabbar's manager back in the States. Jabbar, at the peak of his profession, is about as heavily insured as the Crown Jewels. When his manager heard he had been spending his Hong Kong holiday sparring with Bruce Lee, he had apoplexy. Jabbar's departure heralded not only the end of his cameo role, but also the suspension of the whole project. Lee's international fame suddenly caught up with him with a vengeance. As *The Big Boss* - followed by *Fist of Fury* - stomped across first Europe then America, rewriting box office receipt books and stringing queues of fans five deep around city blocks, producers from Hollywood to Hungary began falling over themselves to sign up the Little Dragon. For Lee, it was as if the heavens had suddenly opened, raining contracts down on him like hailstones. For years he had found it impossible to break down the racial prejudices of the West - and Hollywood in particular. Now he was at the centre of a whirlwind.

At the head of this million dollar queue stood Warner Bros. Warner's production executive Fred Weintraub flew to Hong Kong to offer Concord the chance to co-produce "the first martial arts film made by an American company", as the studio publicity machine later dubbed the venture. It was an offer Lee and Chow could not refuse. Although the total budget for the film - to be called *Enter the Dragon* - was just $600,000, a fraction of the cost of most full-scale Hollywood projects, by Hong Kong standards, it was astronomical. Obviously, Warners were offering Lee the chance of capturing the West, lock, stock and barrel. It was his biggest break yet and he was wildly enthusiastic. *Game of Death* was postponed indefinitely.

PLOTS AND PLANS

"At present, I am working on the script for my next film. I haven't really decided on the title yet, but what I want to show is the necessity to adapt oneself to changing circumstances. The inability to adapt brings destruction. I already have the first scene in my mind. As the film opens, the audience sees a wide expanse of snow. Then the camera closes in on a clump of trees while the sounds of a strong gale fills the screen.

"There is a huge tree in the centre of the screen and it is all covered with thick snow. Suddenly there is a loud snap and a huge branch of the tree falls to the ground. It cannot yield to the force of the snow so it breaks. Then the camera moves to a willow tree which is bending with the wind. Because it adapts itself to the environment, the willow survives.

"It is this sort of symbolism which I think Chinese action films should seek to have. In this way, I hope to broaden the scope of action films."

When Bruce Lee said these words to a newspaper interviewer in Hong Kong, his next film was *The Way of the Dragon*. However, it is more than safe to assume that he was thinking of the film which would later become *Game of Death*. The story that Lee evolved echoed precisely these words, a story highlighting the necessity for adaption and change, specifically in the realm of martial arts. As such, it was a story summing up virtually the whole of Lee's martial arts career.

Lee began his Kung Fu training under a master of the Wing Chun school of Kung Fu, an old man by the name of Ip Man. Wing Chun is a curious style of Kung Fu which was developed by a woman - Yim Wing Chun - some time between the 16th and 17th centuries as a protest against the more rigid, traditional schools. After studying Kung Fu under a Shaolin

nun, Madam Yim had come to the conclusion that the traditional styles were in danger of being suffocated by their own traditions. She drastically cut the number of katas required, placed the emphasis on close quarter fighting and came up with Wing Chun.

Learning under a Wing Chun master, Bruce was instilled with the knowledge that simplicity and directness were far more useful attributes than an ability to recall hundreds of katas. Under Ip Man, the young Bruce mastered the art of fighting without having to follow a pre-set pattern. In particular, Wing Chun taught Bruce to use an opponent's strength and "bend with the wind," rather than attempt to dominate it. Already, the roots of Game of Death - adapt and yield - were beginning to grow.

But even Wing Chun was too restrictive for Lee. Why not, he thought, throw all style out of the window and try for total fighting freedom? The "style" which he subsequently developed himself was, in fact, no style at all. Jeet Kune Do - The Way of the Intercepting Fist - allowed its disciples to use literally every trick in the book, from Western boxing to wrestling to judo to Thai kick boxing.

"I am no style, but I am all styles," Lee would lecture his pupils. "You don't know what I am going to do. My movement is the result of your movement; my technique is the result of your technique."

In retrospect, it seems certain that this is what Lee was intending to show in *Game of*

Death. All his martial career he had been breaking rules, stepping on the toes of the traditionalists, exhorting martial artists to step through the mass of styles which held them in check. If ever Bruce Lee had a message to pass on to his pupils, this was it. It became his life's work. After his death, it was even rumoured that he had been assassinated by a traditionalist master angered by his "blasphemy." *Game of Death* was to provide living proof of the validity of his belief.

Dan Inosanto, an old friend of Lee's who appeared with him in some of the scenes which were completed for *Game of Death*, once spelled out Bruce's real intentions clearly in an interview with an American martial arts magazine. The point behind *Game of Death* was, he said, that the martial artist had to be better than the martial tradition. All the fighters Lee picked as his opponents in the film depicted a certain tradition.

"Even me," commented Inosanto, who played the part of a Filipino "escrima" in *Game of Death*, "I'm dressed in a typical Muslim outfit. But Bruce Lee wears that yellow outfit and looks like the jet set, modern. Everybody else is in traditional garb. Again, his thing is bringing out the greatest thing is to be better than the tradition."

As Inosanto himself pointed out, Lee's other films all carried messages for the martial artist. For instance, the epic Coliseum battle with Churck Norris in *The Way of the Dragon* showed how being a practical fighter is often not enough. Initially, Lee appears to be los-

ing to Norris because he is fighting in a purely practical fashion. It is only when he switches to what Inosanto labelled an "offset" rhythm that he begins to get the upper hand. What was different about *Game of Death*, however, was that Lee appears to have balanced the entire film upon his philosophical message of "adapt and bend."

So far as can be judged from what he said before his death and from the footage that he did manage to capture, this is what Bruce Lee had in mind as the story line of *Game of Death*.

A national treasure is stolen and spirited away to Korea where it is hidden on the top floor of a pagoda-style temple. This pagoda is, in fact, a training school for martial artists of differing styles, and each floor is given over to students of the various forms of defence. The first floor is ruled by a Karateka guard; the second by a hapkido exponent; the third by a Kung Fu disciple; the fourth by the escrima and the fifth and final floor by a fighter whose style is as close to Bruce Lee's Jeet Kune Do as possible. That is, it encompasses all the other styles but also supersedes them. Bruce Lee, accompanied by four other martial artists, travels to the island on which the pagoda stands, fights his way through the various floors - meeting finally with the giant Kareem Adbul-Jabbar who is the Master of the Unknown - and wins back the treasure. To ensure that no guns or weapons are used and that the action relies entirely on martial expertise, metal detectors scan the island.

It was all there - the fighter unburdened by restrictions taking on the traditionalists and beating them into the ground. As a climax, Bruce had planned a twist to put a real sting on the tail of his plot - Lee, the master of Jeet Kune Do, master of the "anything goes" style versus Kareem Abdul-Jabbar, master of no style, just master of himself. On this final, fifth floor, both sides threw away the rule books and relied entirely on their own native, natural skills, man-to-man! Some fight! Some film!

THE CELLULOID BATTLEFIELD

The Way of the Dragon pointed the way for Bruce Lee when he sat down to plan *Game of Death* in more ways than one, not the least being the choice of actors and actresses to fill the pagoda's lethal levels. In his third film, Lee had packed his cast list with genuine top-level martial artists in preference to actors. Consequently, it included such fighting talents as Yang Sze (Bolo Yeung), Shotokan champion of South East Asia, and Chuck Norris seven-time Karate champion. This move towards authenticity rather than good acting paid huge dividends for Lee; indeed his epic battle with Norris must be one of the most gripping action episodes ever filmed.

This casting policy was carried over from *The Way of the Dragon* to *Enter the Dragon*. On Lee's insistence, such martial masters as Bob Wall, Angela Mao and Jim Kelly were included, along with a host of other martial artists drawn from all over the globe. Even co-star John Saxon - better known to film fans for his good looks than his fast fists - was a Kung Fu enthusiast.

Lee was determined that expertise would continue to be the hallmark of his films and to this end he envisaged *Game of Death* as a sort of celluloid battlefield for the cream of the world's martial masters. It was his wish that the film would sponsor the most glittering array of fighters ever assembled.

Kareem Abdul-Jabbar was perhaps little more than a casting department's happy accident - the right man on the right spot at the right time. The other stars of *Game of Death*, however, were chosen after much deep thought by Lee. Unfortunately, what roles they were to play Lee more often than not kept to himself. One star we are certain about though is Dan Inosanto, whose role as keeper of the fourth floor was one of the three fight scenes to be fully completed before Lee's death.

Inosanto first met Bruce Lee in 1964 at a Californian martial arts demonstration. At this time, Inosanto was proficient in a number of the arts, notably Korean, Okinawan and Japanese karate. He was introduced to escrima by Ed Parker, the grand old man of American martial arts. Inosanto studied under escrima's finest masters in both California and Hawaii - names which included the likes of Angel Cabales, Max Sarmiento, Braulio Pedoy and Subing Subing. In time he also had mastered the art.

Escrima (together with its variants kali and amis) is the ancient Filipino art of stick fighting. Today, its development has led it into the realms of sword and dagger combat, but essentially its basis is the block and attack movements of the staff. The art was named by the Spanish conquerors - escrima, meaning skirmish - before they realised its lethal power and banned it. In the north Philippines the movements were kept alive in dance form. In the muslim region in the south, the natives repelled the conquerors and continued the art intact. Today it still survives unchanged in the south were the muslims, still a rebellious and proud people, are conducting a bitter and bloody civil war against the central Filipino Grovernment.

In *Game of Death*, Danny Inosanto wears the costume of a muslim escrima, notable for its Moro headband. Although escrima has in recent years been some-what swamped by the popularity of Kung Fu, another film besides *Game of Death* has been made highlighting the art - The Pacific Connection.

After their meeting in 1964, Bruce and Danny became close friends and several years

later began seriously studying together. When Bruce landed the part of Kato in the Twentieth Century Fox series *The Green Hornet*, he had a lot of time on his hands to devote to Kung Fu and training with him. Inosanto stood in for actor Mako Iwamatsu in one *Green Hornet* episode, titled The Preying Mantis.

In Hong Kong, when Lee was putting together a cast list for *Game of Death*, he immediately thought of his old friend Inosanto as the guardian of one of the pagoda floors. He forwarded a China Airlines ticket to Inosanto, who flew out as soon as he could manage leave from his physical education teaching duties. He remembers how Linda, Bruce's pretty American wife, met him at Kai Tak airport because "Bruce always got mobbed." Within a day, the two men were hard at work.

The third and final fight sequence to be completed was the Hapkido bout with Ji Han Jae, a seventh degree black belt. Unfortunately little is known about this episode, except that two of Bruce's allies are killed by Ji Han Jae before he manages to overcome the Hapkido master. Hapkido, like escrima, is another non-Chinese martial art, hailing originally from Korea. Actually it has only recently been formalised from a mass of ancient Korean teachings dating back some thirteen hundred years. Although its origins are rather obscure, it appears certain that the dreaded Harang Do, the samurai-style knights of ancient Korea, included it in their arsenal. Later, the art was carried on by islolated monks who, forbidden by the emperors to carry arms, used it as a defence technique. Modern Hapkido relies much on high kicks which means that physical perfection is a must.

It is interesting to note that besides

WHO KILLED BRUCE LEE

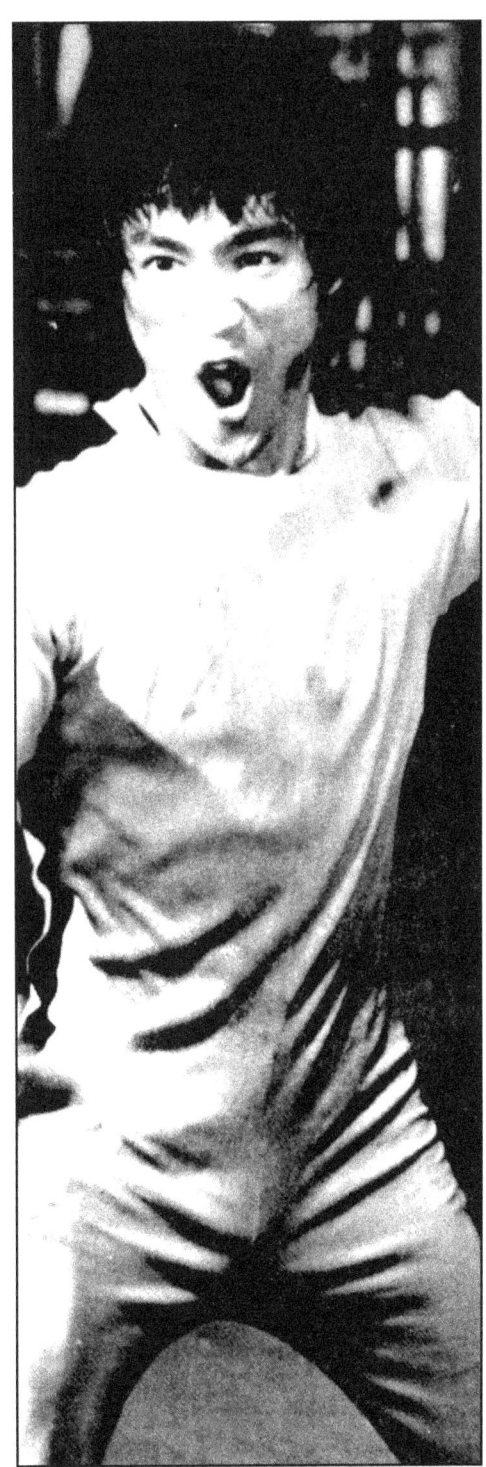

Ji Han Jae, Lee considered a second Hapkido expert for a part in *Game of Death*, the now-famous 'Lady Whirlwind,' Angela Mao. Angela, another Golden Harvest discovery, has, more than any single person, played a leading role in exporting Hapkido to the West and popularising it there. She began her martial film career in the Golden Harvest production *Angry River* and followed it up with the aptly named and enormously successful *Hap Ki Do*. However, the role most Westerners will remember her in is as Bruce Lee's little sister in *Enter the Dragon*. Since then, she has completed a number of films for Golden Harvest - *Deep Thrust*, *Hand of Death*, *Back Alley Princess* and *The Fate of Lee Khan*. All have proved box office hits both in the Far East and West. Now she is one of Hong Kong's top three actresses. This year, Golden Harvest plan to promote her even harder as the star of their martial extravaganza *The Himalayan*. Although no-one knows what Bruce Lee had in mind for her in *Game of Death*, one thing is certain she would not have failed his judgement.

For the rest of the planned cast, their roles can only be guessed at. Shotokan champion Yang Sze, who appeared as the Han's henchman in *Enter the Dragon*, was scheduled to appear and it is not unreasonable to assume that he would have been given the part of master of the first floor, the karateka. Bruce's real-life girlfriend, Betty Ting Pei, was also to have received a role. As revealed in Hong Kong, she was also to have had a part in *Enter the Dragon*, but, "I got sick and my mother sent me to the hospital." However, she too was not told what her part was to be.

Other martial artists and actors reportedly due to appear were Whang In-Sik, James Tien, Jhoon Rhee, Sammo Hung Kam-Po and, apparently, Chuck Norris himself.

The biggest name in acting circles to appear was that of George Lazenby, the Australian actor who shot overnight from male modelling and TV commercial making into Sean Connery's shoes as the "new James Bond". Lazenby had been hanging around in California when one day he had chanced to wander into a local movie house showing Bruce Lee's *Fist of Fury*. According to Lazenby, he was so knocked out by what he saw he "caught the next plane to Hong Kong" and negotiated a part in *Game of Death*.

Taky Kimura, another old friend of Bruce's from the American years, was also offered a part. Now an instructor in Seattle and today considered the world's leading Jeet Kune Do practitioner, Taky received a ticket to Hong Kong in his post box out of the blue. Taky rang Bruce, who explained he wanted him for *Game of Death*. At first Taky declined, saying he was no film star. However Bruce replied, "Everybody looks good in my films," and Taky just had to agree. Twelve hours later, he answered the phone only to learn Bruce Lee was dead.

ACTION

Game of Death was without a shadow of a doubt strictly a one-man show. And that man, of course, was Bruce Lee himself. "His movie-making is like his fighting," Dan Inosanto said recently. "He just did it. He didn't know until the night before exactly what he was going to do. Then he put it together. He made up the story details as he went along, spontaneously. That's the way *Game of Death* was." As Inosanto noted, most of Bruce Lee's movies came from inside Bruce Lee's head, and in *Game of Death* this unique style of film-making was taken to its extreme. Lee had been given a totally free hand with *Way of the Dragon* and he had revelled in the experience. *Enter the Dragon*, following hard

WHO KILLED BRUCE LEE

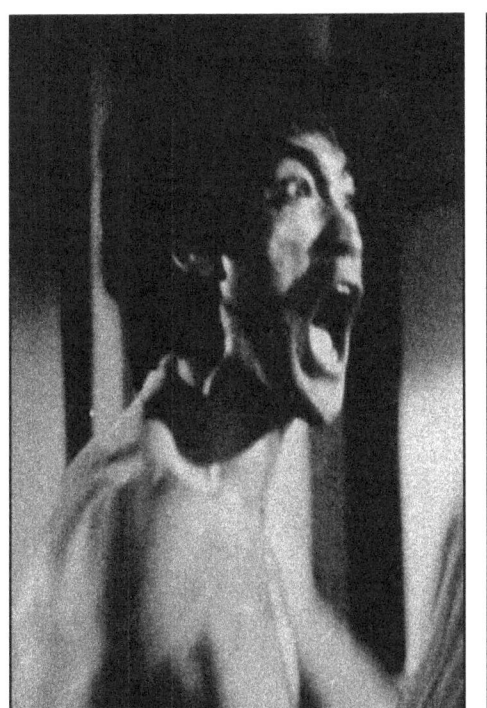

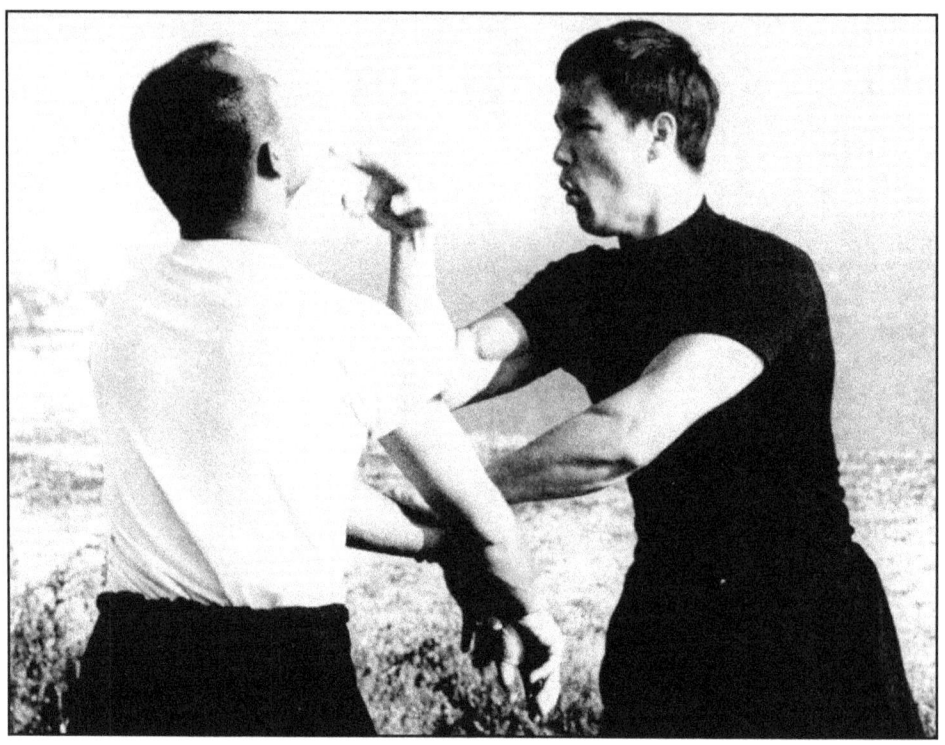

on the heels of *The Way of the Dragon*, must have come as a big anti-climax for the Little Dragon, what with having to once again buckle under to a script-writer, director, cameraman and so on. With *Game of Death* he was breathing free air again. Everything could be done exactly as he wished it.

It would seem perhaps that working with such a dictator might try the patience and temper of even the most good natured actor or actress. Not content with just outlining what was required, Lee would put a performer through his or her paces all the while shouting directions from the sidelines. Because the soundtrack of Hong Kong films is always dubbed in latter, he could work like the silent directors of old, coaching actors even as the cameras turned for a final take.

It would certainly seem to be an off-putting experience filming under the directon of Mr. Lee, but in fact Danny Inosanto, making his first-ever full-length film, said it was in fact quite the opposite. When he first arrived, Danny was one nervous martial artist, afraid that he would "foul-up" a Bruce Lee movie. However, immediately his friend put him at ease. Shortly after Danny's arrival, Bruce began outlining the fight plans he had churning around in his head. For the first three or four days, the two men rehearsed the details with Bruce using a video-tape machine (a technique he had pioneered during his *Green Hornet* days). What he did was to film a rehearsal with video and then play it back immediately. What he wanted was not only the best martial skills, but also the movements that would show up best on camera. As Inosanto later commented, "He was a genius."

In time, Bruce and Danny had worked out the basis of the escrima bout. The sequence starts off with the escrima putting one of Bruce's allies out of action. After he is dragged from the floor, Bruce and Danny get down to it. Three weapons are used during the episode. First up, the escrima chooses the double sticks and Bruce a Chinese bako, a thin whiplike staff of bamboo. Using the bako, Bruce disarms the escrima, who then picks up the nunchakus. Bruce follows suit and the two fight a nunchaku duel to the death. By all accounts the entire episode, titled The Temple of the Tiger, equals any battle Bruce Lee ever filmed. As a tribute to the escrima's courage and martial skill, Lee lets him die a hero.

As many of Lee's associates have also mentioned, Inosanto noted that Bruce was, above all else, a perfectionist. During both rehearsals and final takes he demanded total attention from his actors. When he was given it, he would create scenes at a furious pace, always getting the best out of the people and material at hand. "Bruce was an expert with material for his films," Inosanto recalled after the Little Dragon's death. "Especially in the fight scenes. He could develop it for people who did not know how to fight. Bruce made everyone look good. For those of us who were martial artists, he had a challenge - to make us all look even better. And he always succeeded."

Apparently Kareem Abdul-Jabbar found working under Bruce Lee equally stimulating and rewarding. Although a novice at the martial arts, he and Bruce devised a sequence titled The Temple of the Unknown, which promised to be as breath-taking as it is bizarre. The sequence opens with Bruce and his last remaining ally bursting into the top floor of

the pagoda to face Jabbar, the fighter of the unknown style. Jabbar defeats Bruce's aide and hurls him to the floor below. Then these two extraordinay opponents begin their deadly combat. Stills from the film highlight just how bizarre the match is - when he kicks, Jabbar's enormous foot scythes the air several feet above Bruce's head! Bruce, of course, is the eventual victor.

These then, together with the Hapkido sequence, were the three episodes completed before death intervened. Just how long they run for is still something of a mystery: Dan Inosanto remembers being told that a bare twenty-eight minutes of footage was available. Sources in London claim that at least half the film was completed. When we travelled to Hong Kong, we were informed by a Golden Harvest representative that footage lasting longer than a whole film had been shot and that all that was needed to finish it for release was a series of linking sequences. Whatever the case, the scenes Bruce did manage to capture on celluloid will be well worth seeing even if there are only twenty-eight minutes worth of them. As Dan Inosanto said when it came to producing action films, Bruce Lee was a genius!

END OF THE GAME

On the evening of July 20th 1973, Bruce Lee and Raymond Chow arrived at Betty Ting Pei's Kowloon apartment. They were there to discuss Betty's role in *Game of Death*. After many months, *Enter the Dragon* had been given its final touches and was now waiting to go out on release. Bruce's mind was now firmly fixed on picking up where he had left off on *Game of Death*. He was confident that, whereas his last solo film (*The Way of the Dragon*) had been made really only for an Asian audience, *Game of Death* would prove to the world - and Hong Kong film makers in particular - that Chinese films could be made which would overwhelm both ends of the market - East and West.

A few days earlier, George Lazenby had arrived in Hong Kong, and after the visit to

WHO KILLED BRUCE LEE

Betty's apartment, Bruce and Raymond Chow planned to have dinner with the Australian actor to discuss his role in *Game of Death*. Sometime during the course of the evening, Bruce complained of a headache. Betty told him to lie down and gave him a sleeping pill to help ease the pain. Before he fell asleep, Bruce told Raymond Chow to go on ahead to the restaurant and he would meet him later. In a few short hours, Bruce Lee was dead. Triggered by the sleeping pill Betty had given him, his brain had suffered a seizure - the second in a matter of months - and he had died without gaining consciousness.

When the news broke that Bruce Lee, the fittest man in the world, had died at the incredible age of thirty-two, Hong Kong and the rest of the Far East could not believe its ears. One popular rumour which surfaced immediately and swept a dozen Eastern countries was that it was all just a publicity stunt cooked up to promote *Game of Death*. "The fans have been entering heated arguments over the issue and even placing bets," reported one local newspaper. In time, however, an autopsy was conducted. An inquiry was held to halt the avalanche of rumours, intrigue and innuendo surrounding his death, and eventually a verdict was given: death by misadventure. Bruce Lee, it was decided, had been hypersensitive to the sleeping pill Betty had given him.

That was the clinical report. However, perhaps the cause of his death is more related to what his mother said when she heard the news: "Too much work." Bruce's wife Linda seems to support this theory in her biography of Bruce. In her book, she says that Bruce had come to believe that the only relaxation he could enjoy was more work. "I know John Saxon took the view that Bruce's life was just spiralling away," she writes, "that he had reached a point where he no longer had a goal, that he was just going to go on without ever knowing how high he was going. The strain was there. And the moods were there. I saw his difficulties and I did my best not to add to the stress and strain."

Perhaps it was the very perfectionism which Danny Inosanto and so many others noticed, the quest for perfection which kept Lee going at such a furious pace, that eventually burned him out and cut short his life at such a tragically young age. One after another, he had churned out his films, going faster and faster each time. Perhaps *Game of Death* was the straw which broke the camel's back.

One incident from this period stands out as an example of the pressures Lee was undergoing having jumped from *Enter the Dragon* straight back into the thick of *Game of Death*. Ever since *The Big Boss*, Lee and director Lo Wei had been engaged in a running feud centering on artistic and ego differences. Just a few weeks before his death, Bruce arrived at the Golden Harvest studio to run through the *Game of Death* plot with Raymond Chow. Learning that Lo Wei was in a nearby screening room, Lee suddenly erupted and rushed in to tell the startled director what he thought of him. The matter was not resolved until the police had been called and Bruce had signed a slip of paper promising in writing to leave Lo Wei alone.

Besides providing incredible work pressures on Bruce, *Game of Death* was also blamed in a more straightforward fashion by the Chinese community for Bruce's death. The Chinese have a long tradition of supersititious belief - known as Feng Shui - and the film's title was, to the Chinese fans, an obvious bad luck symbol. It was reported that when the title was first thought of, Lo Wei, recalling a top Chinese actor who had died in a car crash ten years previously after filming a movie titled *Rendezvous with Death*, warned that *Game of Death* was tempting fate.

THE FUTURE

With the grief and controversy over Lee's death raging throughout the Far East, *Game of Death* was somehow lost in the uproar. For months it lay forgotten in the Golden Harvest archives while the world debated the facts surrounding Lee's tragic demise. For any other actor, death would spell the end of big box office pulling power. But with Lee, it acted in the reverse: overnight he crossed the line from millionaire actor to mysterious legend. Throughout the West the lines outside the cinemas swelled to their largest ever. The Bruce Lee cult had begun.

With such extraordinary public appeal being generated by Bruce's movies both at home and abroad, it was, naturally enough, not long before Raymond Chow began thinking about releasing *Game of Death*. What with fans packing out showings of *Marlowe*, a B-grade Hollywood detective story starring James Garner in which Lee appeared for about five short minutes as an oriental villain, Chow must certainly have realised that a "new Bruce Lee film," even if it contained only twenty-eight minutes of Bruce himself, would have caused a sensation. However, *Game of Death* remained on the shelf. Indeed, it was to be a full three years before the threads were finally taken up once again.

There are a number of reasons why *Game of Death* was neglected for so long. According to several sources in Hong Kong, the main stumbling block for many months was the name of the film itself. Linda Lee objected - quite understandably - to the inclusion of the word "death" in the title. Raymond Chow, on the other hand, was convinced that, from a business point of view, *Game of Death* was the only title that was acceptable. *Game of Death* was what the fans knew. It was what they were expecting. Any other title would have caused confusion. Chow was even more convinced as to the validity of his argument when a sudden spate of "Bruce Lee" imitations began to flood the market. Using doubles, these films purported to tell Lee's life story, usually through a mixture of innuendo and tired old gossip. But one of these imitations went one step further. Titled L*egend of Bruce Lee*, it had a plot line remarkably similar to parts of the *Game of Death* script.

The film opens with the bogus Lee (played by a young actor from Taiwan named Li Roy Lung who has made a recent career out of portraying the Little Dragon) being ushered into a movie screening room by a man closely resembling Raymond Chow. On the screen is another film which is obviously meant to be *Game of Death*. After much incomprehensible coming and going, Lung's girlfriend (who is doubtless meant to be portraying Betty Ting Pei) is kidnapped. Lung changes into a yellow track suit and learns she is being held on the top floor of a pagoda. It is up to Lung to battle his way up each floor to rescue her. One of his opponents just happens to be a very tall black American! With this sort of rip-off film doing the rounds, it must have been an obvious fact in the Golden Harvest boardroom that Game of Death under any other title may very will have been lost in the flood of cheap imitations.

According to American rumours, another stumbling block to the film's early release was Linda's desire to complete her own film biography of Bruce. However, it is difficult to image that Bruce's widow would contemplate holding up the film if it could possibly be completed and released. A much more powerful reason is contained in Linda's book describing her life with Bruce. In the book, she states that, before any movies are made, the problems associated with shooting a large part of the movie without Bruce appearing

WHO KILLED BRUCE LEE

THE KUNG-FU MONTHLY ARCHIVE SERIES

must be overcome. As it stands now, only the fight scenes have been completed. This means that a whole connecting plot must be constructed linking the scenes - all without the Little Dragon. There have been a number of suggestions aimed at surmounting the problem. A double of Bruce could be used, although this seems a very unsatisfactory way of getting around it. After all, Bruce Lee's face is one of the most famous in the world, and to ask an audience to forget who it is they are looking at one moment and then to show them the real thing the next would appear to be stretching reactions to the extreme. Another suggestion is that Bruce's action sequences could be used as the flashbacks in the mind of another, entirely new, hero.

If a double is to be used, one likely candidate for the role is a young martial artist by the name of Alex Kwon. First Artists, the Hollywood production company handling Linda Lee's *Tribute to Bruce Lee* spent weeks auditioning martial artists hopeful of stepping into the Little Dragon's celluloid shoes. Unfortunately, no-one could be found to fit the bill. By chance, an editor of a leading American martial arts magazine spotted up-and-coming Kung Fu competitor Alex Kwon wandering through his office one day. The editor was so struck by Kwon's resemblance to Lee that he forwarded him to Hollywood post haste. After throwing the right punches and pulling the proper faces, Kwon was hired. By fortunate coincidence, Kwon's style of martial art - known as my jong law horn - is similar to Jeet Kune Do in that it is extremely fluid. Even though *Tribute to Bruce Lee* has not yet gone into production (it is scheduled for spring shooting), Alex Kwon is already making an impression on the Hollywood backlots. Steve McQueen, who saw Alex work out for his screen test, claims the young martial artist bears an uncanny resemblance to the Little Dragon.

As things stand now, the first steps are now being taken to pull *Game of Death* back into production. As one Golden Harvest spokesman told us in Hong Kong, four scripts have been prepared and submitted to Raymond Chow. If Chow likes one of the four, it will provide the basis for linking Bruce's fight scenes and tying them in to a complete movie. If he rejects them all, a new script will be speedily written by one of the Californian script writers who have been approached by Golden Harvest over the past few weeks. Perhaps sometime in April shooting will commence. Perhaps sometime in autumn, *Game of Death* will be complete.

In Hong Kong recently, a Golden Harvest executive, when asked the reason for the three year delay in reshooting *Game of Death*, paused for a moment and then answered that, although there were other factors, perhaps the biggest reason was that the company felt everything had to be done just right. It was Bruce Lee's last testament, he said, and it had to be remade exactly as he would have wished it. Anything less than perfection would be unforgiveable. Soon the waiting will be over and *Game of Death*, the most fascinating film in recent years, will flash onto cinema screens around the globe. Let's just pray that it is a legacy worthy of the most extraordinary man of our time - Bruce Lee, Little Dragon.

EPILOGUE

Looking back in retrospect from the first anniversary of his death, it seems that almost before Bruce Lee had fully arrived, he was gone. Although a national hero to the Chinese people of the Far East in his own lifetime, the message that he left to them was only crudely and partially formulated, a mere fraction of the potential leadership he undoubtedly possessed. To his Western audiences, he was dead before they ever really came to know him. But in the few short years that Lee grasped the tiger's tail, he forged several indelible thumbprints whose long term social and cultural effects will survive long after his films have dropped into obscurity.

For the Chinese movie industry, from starlet to mogul, the Shockwaves of Lee's demise are still too fresh to afford easy analysis. Certainly Lee was infinitely more than the local boy made good. In many ways he was responsible for shaping both the future internal and external aspirations of the Mandarin film world. His defiance in the face of Run Run Shaw's initial (and to Lee, insulting) offer; his insistence in a percentage cut of profits; his fierce desire to control and supervise every aspect of his own films; these are all innovations that Shaw Bros, and other movie companies can ignore at their peril. As the extent of Lee's demands sinks home in the minds of a new generation of contract actors and actresses, one feels confident in predicting that Movietown and its ilk must eventually adapt to the changing realities of life outside the colony. The days of the Dream Factory are numbered, and it is to Bruce Lee primarily that Mr. Shaw must turn if he seeks to lay his finger on the root cause of the options soon to confront him.

Similarly, Lee's international outlook has widened the horizons and opportunities (not to mention purses), of the Chinese film producers. His golden punch has proved to be the key that has unlocked world wide markets for what only a short time ago could fairly have been described as a profitable but extremely parochial backyard industry. Already, Shaw Bros, and Golden Harvest are pooling their resources with overseas film companies from America, Britain and Italy, and co-producing internationally orientated features along the

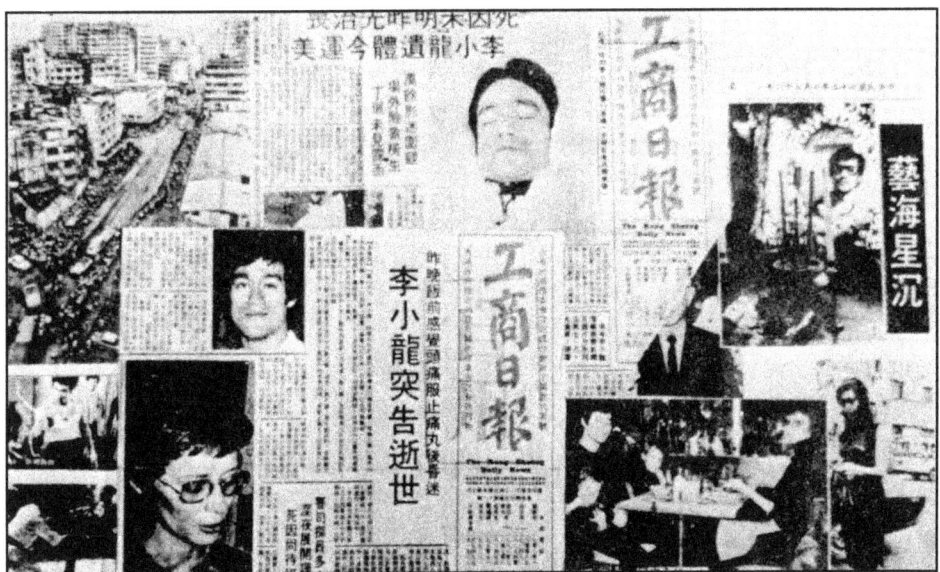

lines of the *Enter the Dragon* partnership. Chinese film production, post Bruce Lee, is now on a grand scale.

As a martial artist, Lee singlehandedly inspired and ignited the Oriental combat craze currently gripping a dozen countries both East and West. Precisely at the moment that the Western world began turning Eastwards on an increasing number of fronts, in politics, philosophy and medicine, Lee consciously assumed the role of spokesman for an almost unknown system of defence, and thereby captured the attention, minds and bodies of countless thousands of martial arts enthusiasts. Inspired (and perhaps to some extent goaded), by his own boyhood experiences on the streets, Lee adapted this system to 20th Century urban requirements. Today, as with its predecessor Karate, Kung Fu has so entrenched itself in the lives of young people from New York to New Delhi, that what was once heralded as just another craze seems almost certain to have permanent repercussions. David Carradine and television's *Kung Fu* notwithstanding; Kung Fu is Bruce Lee's revolution.

In the red light district of Wanchai, a Hong Kong suburb known as the Brothel of the Orient, a strange new hoarding now jostles for a place amongst the neon advertisements illuminating sex sauna baths and Topless-Chinese-Girls-A-Go-Go. Smiling faintly down upon the streets and alleys he once roamed as a teenage hoodlum, is Bruce Lee's memorial - a gigantic photographic enlargement of the charismatic King of Kung Fu. Written across it in Chinese characters as an inspiration and reminder for the prostitutes, pimps, fans and tourists beneath, is the simple legend:

THE SPIRIT OF BRUCE LEE LIVES ON

THE BOB BAKER LETTERS

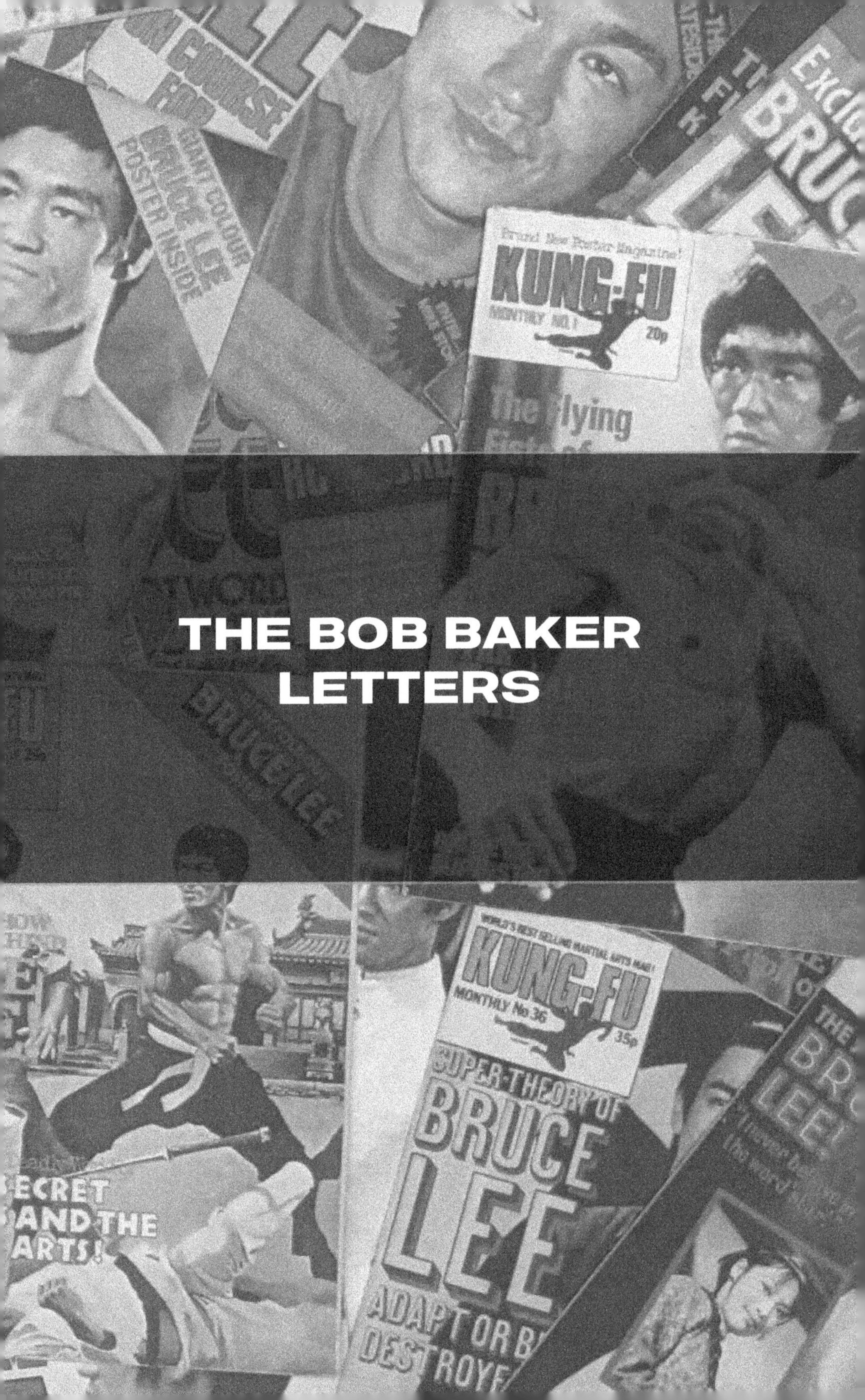

"The goodies list can be: (1) COKE (in large amount), (2) ACID (in fair amount), (3) HASH OR GRASS (the former can be more while the latter, even cleaned, has to be carefully packed."

- Bruce Lee to Bob Baker (1972)

"Bob, Bruce wants you to see if you can get some coc[sic]"

- Linda Lee to Bob Baker (June 1972)

WHO KILLED BRUCE LEE

To his millions of fans, he was the epitome of martial arts. Hailed as one of the fittest men on the planet and the founder of modern-day mixed martial arts, he was the undisputed martial arts master. After dismissing traditional styles of martial arts as a "classical mess," Lee developed his own personal fighting philosophy, which, in Cantonese, he called Jeet Kune Do or The Way of the Intercepting Fist as translated into English. After his tragic death in 1973 at the age of just 32, his full recognition in the western world came posthumously. His image is as iconic as that of Marilyn Monroe or James Dean and is instantly recognisable the world over. His recent portrayal by Mike Moh in Quentin Tarantino's latest movie *Once Upon a Time... in Hollywood*, was received negatively by his fans, his family and race equality campaigners. A fitness fanatic throughout his life, Lee barely ever drank alcohol or touched drugs, therefore it was a major shock at the coroner's inquiry when it was revealed that a small amount of cannabis was found in his stomach as the time of his death. The Hong Kong newspapers at the time had a field day, though it was later suggested that Lee was introduced to the drug by his friend, the actor, James Coburn and that he used it occasionally to relax from a heavy and stressful work schedule. After all, from 1971 to his death in 1973, Lee had completed four films, four episodes of a TV show and was a third of the way through his unfinished masterpiece *The Game of Death*. Two of the films saw him not only take on the lead acting role, but he was also the writer, director and producer. The impact of his cannabis use revelation eventually died down with time.

In the years that followed his death, his fanbase of dedicated fans has waned, yet his popularity, promoted through his "brand," has only increased.

The fact that Bruce Lee is portrayed as a clean-cut fitness fanatic and martial arts master, makes it unfathomable to believe that in addition to the 1973 cannabis revelation, newly surfaced letters present Lee as a secret cocaine, magic mushroom and LSD user. Written to his friend Bob Baker, the letters show Lee updating his friend on his progressing career, but also present a darker side with Lee ordering drugs several times to be shipped to him through the postal service. Bob Baker was raised in Stockton, California and was a student at Lee's Jun Fan Gung Fu School in Oakland, California in 1964. In 1972, Lee got his friend a small role as a Russian enforcer named Petrov in his second major Hong Kong film, Fist of Fury. After filming *Fist of Fury* and as his fame grew, a paranoid Lee recruited Baker as an unofficial part-time bodyguard. The collection of almost fifty letters written to Baker from Bruce and his wife Linda have recently come up for auction in the USA and as well as revealing a close friendship, they harbour darker tones.

After a meeting between Lee and Baker at an unknown date, Lee writes, "It was a brief but definitely enjoyable get together. Thank you again for this 'holy stuff.'" What the 'holy stuff' is, isn't revealed but it is mentioned by Lee in another letter from around 1971 after Lee returned from a stay at The Dorchester hotel in London, where he had a meeting with Coburn and the producer Stirling Silliphant to discuss their plans for their then-upcoming movie project, *The Silent Flute*. Lee, offered to purchase some of the substance with Baker and wrote, "By the way, wouldn't mind going in with you for some of those 'holy stuff' before leaving for H.K."

Another letter mentions that Lee would, "... like to store up on some 'holy stuff' to bring over there," and that Baker should, "See if you can come up with something good." Another letter also suggests that actor James Coburn was also involved with the usage of

THE KUNG-FU MONTHLY ARCHIVE SERIES

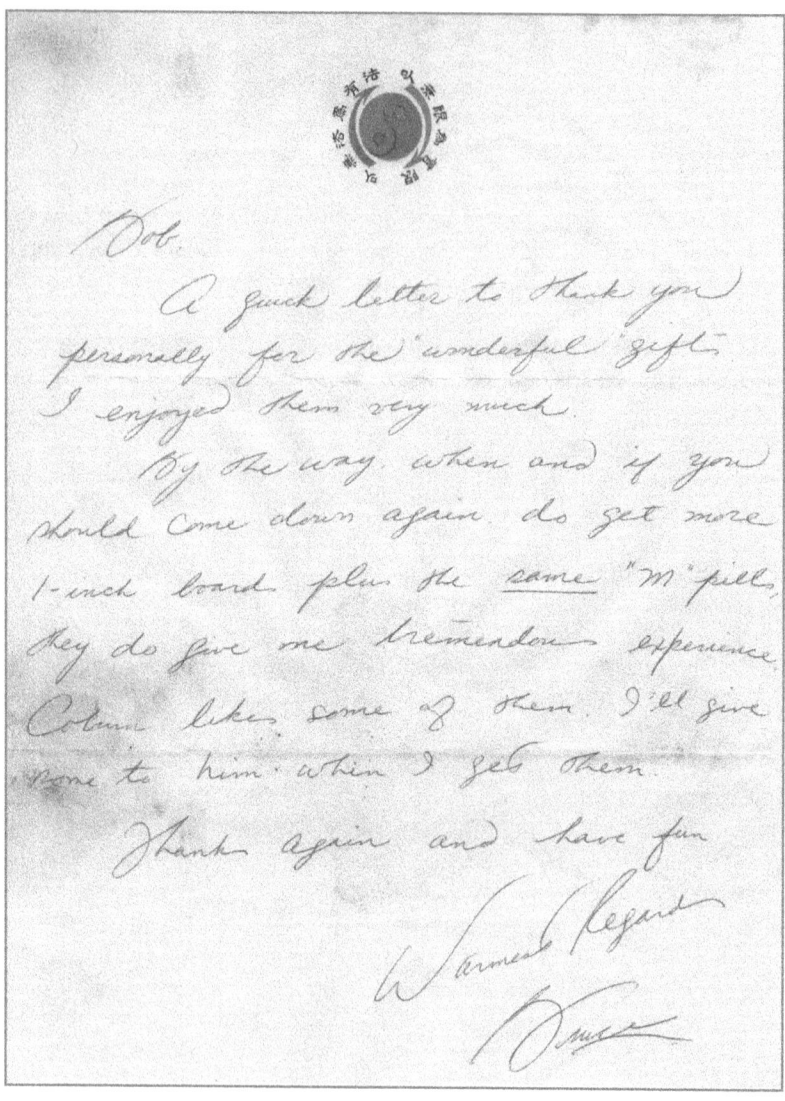

Letter from Bruce Lee to Bob Baker postmarked 22 April 1970 requesting 'M' pills, which were likely to be a hynotic sedative called Methaqualone or Quaaludes (nicknamed Mandrakes or Mandies in the US). Whilst not an illegal substance at the time, the drug was more tightly regulated in Britain under the Misuse of Drugs Act 1971 and in the U.S. from 1973. It was withdrawn from many developed markets in the early 1980s. In the United States it was withdrawn in 1983 and made a Schedule I drug in 1984.

Bruce Lee and Bob Baker during a scene at the end of Fist of Fury.

Baker's supplies as Lee wrote, "By the way, when and if you do get more 1-inch boards plus the same 'M' pills, they do give me tremendous experience. Coburn likes some of them. I'll give some to him when I get them." The M-pills that Lee requested were Methaqualone or Quaaludes and were popular in the 1970s with the hippy and glam rock communities. They were something crushed and smoked with cannabis though Lee probably wouldn't have done so as he never smoked, though that could be questioned as an undated letter reveals, "A personal letter to thank you for bringing me the stuffs, especially the pipe and the painting."

In another letter, Lee appears to have tried steroids or something similar but didn't wish to carry on taking them as he felt that, "...excessive indulgence of them just isn't in my road in Jeet Kune Do." In a letter written to Baker shortly before he would start filming his directorial debut, *The Way of the Dragon* in 1972, Lee signed off by asking, "By the way, what is the advice on the possibility of getting some coke over to me?"

One letter suggests that during one of Baker's visits, Lee became so high that he couldn't even remember what happened during their time together. As Lee wrote, "Though I have little recollection of what has happened...... anyway, I know that you enjoyed your stay and am looking forward for another visit from you. Thank you for that stuffs and do take care and have fun."

In a letter date stamped February 28, 1972, after Lee relocated to Hong Kong due to the success of his first film *The Big Boss*, he tells Baker, "Still am in the process of adapting to life here. By the way, what is the advice in the possibility of shipping some coke to me?"

In an undated letter, Lee writes, "Bob, Air-mail me some Coca-Cola - do it the way you and I sincerely feel - in other words, whatever. Be cool about the package, same procedure Wu Ngan - 'quality! man.' What more can I say but I care for you - be careful and take good care. Love & Peace, Bruce." Though undated, the letter is from mid 1972 as the P.S.

> Dear Bob and Ben,
>
> June 2, 1972
>
> Bruce asked me to write and send this check to you because you have always been a good, true friends and because you really helped us out when we needed it. We hope it will help you while you are getting started in the tree trimming business.
>
> Bruce is very very busy right now, so I'm writing for him because he wants to keep in touch and he's concerned about how you're doing. We hope everyone in the family is fine. By the way, Brandon says hello to Dale and Laurie.

> Bruce just got back from two weeks in Rome. Today they started shooting at the studio, and will continue straight through till the film is done. We have seen the film that they shot in Rome, and as you can guess, Bruce is doing great in his first directing job. Chuck Norris & Bob Wall are appearing in this picture.
>
> We bought a house in Kowloon Tong. It is really fantastic. We'll be moving in July 1. Our new address will be: 41 Cumberland Rd. Kowloon Tong Kowloon, Hong Kong

> I'm kind of in a rush today because it's very very hot and I'm taking the kids swimming shortly. So, one last thing regarding the cats: if they become too much burden for you, housewise, food wise, messwise, and I'm sure that so many cats are a problem, then you don't have to feel that you have to keep them. If you do give them away, try to find good homes, and if possible it would be nice if they would stay together.
>
> Our best to you all,
> Love,
> Linda

> P.S. Bob Bruce wants you to see if you can get some coc. Just see if you can, and then we'll figure out how to send it.

Letter from Linda Lee to Bob Baker dated 2 June 1972. As stated in the letter, Lee was hard at work on his directorial debut, The Way of the Dragon, filming on the Colisseum set at Golden Harvest Studios in Hong Kong after returning from his trip to Italy the month before. As a postscript, Linda requests Baker try to obtain some 'coc' - most likely to be cocaine.

at the end of the letter mentions that Lee's directorial debut, *Way of the Dragon*, is on the way. Wu Ngan was Lee's butler and a family friend from his childhood days. After Lee's death in 1973, some controversy emerged since Lee's own production company Concord - formed in partnership with his Golden Harvest producer Raymond Chow - was in his butler's name, who was the sole beneficiary of what little money Lee had at the time of his death. The cannabis revelation at his inquest almost stopped Lee's insurance pay-out to his widow, Linda and she was forced to sell the rights to her late husband's unfinished film, The Game of Death, to his former business partner, Raymond Chow.

In another letter, Lee requested that Baker, "... send some Coke," and stated that he was, "... stoned as hell." He said he was working on an upcoming character and that, "Some coke would help in the formation of what I would like to create."

In another letter, Lee places an order and requests that Baker send it to Golden Harvest Studios on Nathan Road in Hong Kong, and addressed to Wu Ngan. In the letter, Lee orders, "(1) COKE (in large amount), (2) ACID (in fair amount), (3) HASH OR GRASS (the former can be more while the latter, even cleaned, has to be carefully packed." Lee knew what he was doing was illegal and then goes on to instruct Baker how he should package everything together so as not to be discovered. "As to what you put the above with you know better - inside books? Clothes?" At the end of the letter, Lee asks Baker if he can get him some Psilocybin or Magic Mushrooms, "Do you have access to any PSILOCYBIN. If so, send a little together with info on how to take it. Read about it in a book."

Even Lee's wife Linda knew about the illicit drug use. In a three-page letter dated June 2, 1972, Linda explains how Bruce has been working on *Way of the Dragon* with Chuck Norris and Bob Wall and how they'll be shortly moving house, before signing off and adding the P.S., "Bob, Bruce wants you to see if you can get some coc [sic]. Just see if you can, and then we'll figure out how to send it."

In one letter, Lee even jokes that he needs something sending quick, writing, "I hope you will send the 'quality' stuff you said you will send ('it has never been from the street')." And that he should, "... send it 'AIR-MAIL' like yesterday (HA! HA!)"

All of the letters show a tremendous amount of respect and friendship that Lee had for Baker but most turn to the discussion of supplying drugs. For example, one reads, "You take good care of yourself and your family. By the way, I'll be waiting for the 1oz of H. Oil I have ordered from you - send it as soon as you can." The H. Oil referred to was probably Hashish Oil which is similar to the legal CBD Cannabis Oil on sale all over today, the difference being that today's oil removes THC, the psychoactive ingredient that gives the user the "high" they would get from cannabis use.

As well as using the cocaine they were buying, there is a possibility that Bruce and/or Linda were buying it to redistribute. Following on from Bruce's letter, in a letter dated March 29th (1973), Linda writes, "I've bought a gram measurer and enclosed you will find the $500 for the amount of C you quote that Bruce can get. I'll measure it, but the quality (that goes without saying) plus the quantity Bruce himself will have to judge. I hope you will send him the mostest [sic] along with the one oz of H. oil and/or whatever." By purchasing the scales and offering to weigh the C or cocaine out herself, was Linda doing it to split the quantity for personal use of was she doing it to sell on to others? I guess we will never know the answer to that.

Two weeks later on April 14th, Linda wrote to Baker once again. "I assume you have

> Bob,
>
> Just want you to know that Linda had yesterday send the ADDITIONAL money you have requested.
>
> I had a hard day, a REAL HARD day.
>
> You take good care of yourself and your family. By the way, I'll be waiting for the 1 oz of H. oil I have ordered from you — send it as soon as you can.
>
> Peace
>
> Bruce

Though Linda Lee would continue to correspond with Bob Baker in the years to come, this was the final letter Baker would receive from Bruce, postmarked 21 March 1973, whilst Lee was working on Enter the Dragon. Lee's emphasis on sending additional money that Baker had requested and having a hard day gives an insight into the strain that fame was having on the star. The Hashish oil was likely to be used to help Lee relax. Unbeknownst to Baker at the time, was that Lee would trgically pass away some four months later, aged just 32.

received the money order for $500 and I am wondering if you have sent the C yet. Please let me know right away." Linda was fully aware of the risk involved in their activity and acknowledged that in the April 14th letter. "Say thanks to Bev for taking the risk and sending the last shipment to Bruce. Don't worry about Bruce using the C - he is not going overboard.... Write very soon and let us know about the $500 money order and /or when the C is coming."

That letter was the last one Baker would receive in Bruce Lee's lifetime as he would pass away a little over three months later of a cerebral oedema or swelling of the brain at the apartment of young Taiwanese actress Betty Ting Pei, who called Raymond Chow for assistance when she could not wake him after he had gone for a lie down due to a headache. That would have raised some eyebrows itself, but the Hong Kong press ran riot when Linda Lee and Raymond Chow had both knowingly lied by telling the world that Lee had collapsed at his home. The official verdict given by the coroner at the time was "death by misadventure." Linda would continue to write to Baker for some years on a friendship basis until his death in 1993 – a month shy of his 53rd birthday.

The drug references in the letters are a shame, as for Bruce Lee historians, they provide vital information and insight into a time when Bruce Lee went from barely scraping by as a jobbing actor to becoming the biggest superstar that Hong Kong had ever seen and all within a period of six months.

Though the content of the letters may be shocking, perhaps there are valid reasons for his use of the various substances. The cannabis could have been used to treat pain in his back which is referenced in the letters or to treat stress and as stated earlier, to help him to relax. If the cannabis was to help him relax, then perhaps the cocaine was to have the opposite effect and give him energy. Many times in the letters does Lee express how tired he feels about the "silly fighting" he had to do. The time that the letters were written was one of hippies and free love, with LSD, magic mushrooms and other psychedelic drugs being frequently used, especially in Hollywood. Their long-term effects and damage had not been researched at the time. After all, it took over a decade for Quaaludes to be banned in the United States.

While Bruce Lee's daughter Shannon continuously spends her time chastising Quentin Tarantino in countless media articles over the portrayal of her father in his movie, *Once Upon a Time... in Hollywood* and it's subsequent novel, a media storm was brewing elsewhere but somehow, ignoring it, bizarrely meant it went away with little fuss. Newspapers ran stories with headlines such as "Chasing the Dragon" but Linda Lee nor Shannon Lee made a statement to the press regarding the letters to neither confirm or deny them. It was pretty much business as usual for Shannon Lee's powerbrand, Bruce Lee Enterprises; more t-shirts, posters, more sports shoes, more figures, more die cast buses.

The letters, when sold at auction by Heritage Auctions in 2021, netted Bob Baker's descendents over US $470,000 - more than double the estimate. Why Baker kept those letters for twenty years after Lee's passing is anyone's guess; perhaps he wanted to still have something to remember his friend by from a time long gone and simply forgot about them when he passed away in 1993. After all, they were only discovered by Baker's adult children after their mother passed away many years later.

Now that the letters are in the open, only time will tell if they have any bearing on the quest to find out who killed Bruce Lee.

ALSO BY THE AUTHOR

THE K.F.M. BRUCE LEE SOCIETY

"BEAUTIFULLY CAPTURES THE HEART, SOUL, AND SPIRIT OF THE UNITED KINGDOM'S FLEDGLING BRUCE LEE FANBASE. UNDENIABLY COLLECTIBLE."

— BRUCE LEE REVIEW

"NOT JUST A COMPILATION OF NOSTALGIC NEWSLETTERS, BUT A BRITISH HISTORY GUIDE TO A PERIOD TIME WHEN WESTERN PEOPLE DISCOVERED THE UNIQUE TALENTS OF THE UNDISPUTED KING OF KUNG FU - BRUCE LEE."

— ANDREW J. STATON, BRITISH JUN FAN JOURNAL

"THANK YOU VERY MUCH FOR YOUR TIME AND EFFORT TO HONOUR PAM FOR HER GREAT WORK AND DEDICATION. I, TOGETHER WITH THE BRUCE LEE FANS WHO KNEW PAM SALUTE YOU!"

— ROBERT LEE

THE **KUNG-FU MONTHLY** BRUCE LEE SECRET SOCIETY BEGAN IN SEPTEMBER 1976, RUNNING FOR 30 ISSUES BEFORE IT'S FINAL ISSUE IN SEPTEMBER 1983. RUN BY THE FORMIDABLE PAM HADDEN, THE BRUCE LEE SECRET SOCIETY FUNCTIONED AS THE SOURCE OF INFORMATION FOR BRUCE LEE FANS IN THE UK AND LATER, THE REST OF THE WORLD. FOR THE FIRST TIME EVER, ALL 30 ISSUES HAVE BEEN PAINSTAKINGLY RE-EDITED AND RE-PRINTED IN THIS BOOK, ALONG WITH UPDATED NOTES AND RETROSPECTIVE STORIES BY THE PEOPLE MOST RESPONSIBLE FOR KEEPING BRUCE LEE'S MEMORY ALIVE - THE FANS.

AVAILABLE FROM **WWW.KUNGFUMONTHLY.UK** & AMAZON

THE WORLD FAMOUS MARKETPLACE

DON'T FORGET TO VISIT OUR WEBSITE FOR OTHER FANTASTIC ITEMS INCLUDING CLOTHING AND LIMITED EDITION SETS!

◄ BRUCE LEE KING OF KUNG FU

Written by Felix Dennis & Don Atyeo, Bruce Lee King of Kung Fu is the original and still one of the greatest books on Bruce Lee ever written. Packed with photos and essential information from the immediate year after Lee's tragic death, Bruce Lee King of Kung Fu provides the best of rock-solid backgrounds to the story of the man we all know and love.
170 PAGES

BUY ONLINE NOW!

amazon
WHSmith
Waterstones

OR VISIT OUR WEBSITE AT
WWW.KUNGFUMONTHLY.UK

KUNG-FU MONTHLY ► THE POSTER MAGAZINES

Volume One - No. 1 to 25, trade dummy plus an in-depth article on The History of Kung-Fu Monthly 1973 to 1979.
Volume Two - No. 26 to 55 plus interviews with former KFM staff.
Volume Three - No. 56 to 79, double-poster special edition issue plus an in-depth article on The History of Kung-Fu Monthly 1980 to 1984.
540-670 PAGES

THE BOOK OF ► KUNG FU

The Book of Kung Fu was to be Kung-Fu Monthly's special annual issue, but was only published in 1974. Over one-hundred pages, many of them in colour, with a durable soft cover and scores of photographs, illustrations and articles. Don't miss this book! Bruce Lee, Angela Mao, David Carradine, Kung Fu Quiz, Comic Book and more - an incredible publication!
144 PAGES

THE SECRET ART OF ► BRUCE LEE

In 1976, the world took its first look at the now legendary Chester Maydole photographs. Arranged where possible, in 'fast-frame' action sequences, The Secret Art of Bruce Lee shows the founder of Jeet Kune Do, assisted by his friend and student Dan Inosanto, demonstrating the early development state of his art Jeet Kune Do during early days in Los Angeles.
110 PAGES

THE LOST KFM BOOK
FIRST TIME EVER IN THE UK!

◄ THE WISDOM OF BRUCE LEE

The Wisdom of Bruce Lee was to be one of the first books in the world to look at Bruce Lee's philosophy on life and martial arts. Mysteriously never released in the UK, The Wisdom of Bruce Lee is finally available to UK Bruce Lee fans after a wait of over forty years.
The full-length version includes a new introduction and interview with author Roger Hutchinson by Jun Fan Journal writer Andrew Staton, while the shorter abridged version is formatted in the style of the original Kung-Fu Monthly books.
70 PAGES / 170 PAGES

◄ THE UNBEATABLE BRUCE LEE

The Unbeatable Bruce Lee presents readers with a fighter's view of Bruce Lee the man and Bruce Lee the martial arts master. Beneath the sheer weight of known facts and figures that surround the tragically short life of Hong Kong's number one son, lies a strata of truth that only now is beginning to be picked.
112 PAGES

◄ BRUCE LEE IN ACTION

With Bruce Lee in Action, the Editors of Kung-Fu Monthly had compiled another fine addition to their library of Bruce Lee publications. Lavishly illustrated throughout with many previously unseen photographs at the time, this informative book investigates clearly and concisely, the birth and subsequent development of Lee's fighting style Jeet Kune Do, both on and off the screen.
106 PAGES

THE POWER OF ► BRUCE LEE

Bruce Lee was possibly the greatest exponent of the martial arts ever produced. The fact that he was a movie star often clouds his enormous contribution to the field. The Power of Bruce Lee explores many of his revolutionary methods of attack and defence, especially those relating to Jeet Kune Do, Lee's name for his own fighting system
110 PAGES

WHO KILLED ► BRUCE LEE?

Who Killed Bruce Lee? is a study of the pressures and the forces that, on the one hand were to elevate him to the highest plains of stardom and on the other, were to so tragically strike him down before his final fulfilment.
Who Killed Bruce Lee? was one of the first books to delve deep into the newspaper stories of Lee's early death.
108 PAGES

◀ THE GAME OF DEATH

This book combines two Kung-Fu Monthly special edition magazines released prior to Golden Harvest's 1978 film. Researched exclusively in Hong Kong, Kung-Fu Monthly reports on Lee's plot for Game of Death, the cast he intended to appear in the film, the scenes already filmed and Lee's hopes and expectations for the success of the project. Incredibly accurate for the time, this publication represents an important part of Bruce Lee fandom in the UK.
XXX PAGES

FIND OUT MORE INFORMATION AT

THE MAGAZINES

WWW.KUNGFUMONTHLY.UK

◀ THE BEGINNER'S GUIDE TO KUNG FU

Originally released in 1974, The Beginner's Guide to Kung Fu was the first martial arts book aimed primarily at the Kung Fu Craze generation. The graphic, easy to understand illustrations by Paul Simmons and the carefully conceived step by step instructions made this the perfect book for beginners who wished to take up Kung Fu.
XXX PAGES

▲
THE BRUCE LEE SCRAPBOOK

In 1974, Kung-Fu Monthly issued a Bruce Lee scrapbook in the form of a large A3 magazine, followed by a smaller A4 sized book in 1979. As part of the KFM Archive Series, both scrapbooks have been combined in a new chronological layout with brand new captions, location information and dates by Carl Fox and Jun Fan Journal writer Andrew Staton.
150 PAGES

THE KFM BRUCE LEE SOCIETY ▶

Long before the internet communities we know today, The Bruce Lee Society was the source of information in the United Kingdom for all things Bruce Lee. Now the history of the Bruce Lee Society is finally told in The Bruce Lee Society: A Retrospective Look at Bruce Lee Mania and the Kung Fu Craze of the 1970s. For the first time ever, all thirty issues of The Bruce Lee Society newsletters have been painstakingly re-edited and re-printed in this book, along with updated notes and retrospective stories by the people most responsible for keeping Bruce Lee's memory alive - the fans.
544 PAGES

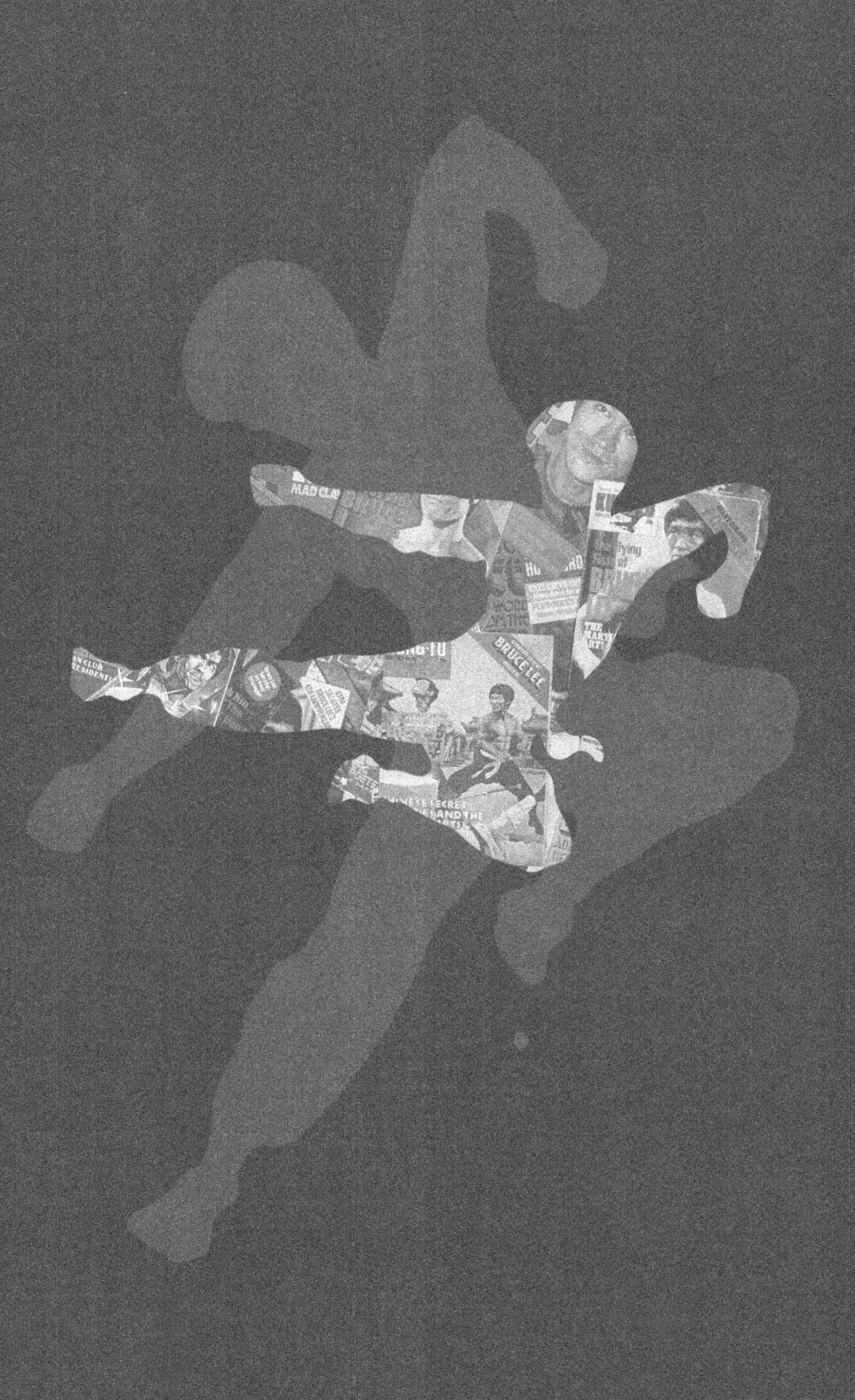

www.ingramcontent.com/pod-product-compliance
Lightning Source LLC
Chambersburg PA
CBHW061227070526
44584CB00029B/4028